ENGLISH in Common

with ActiveBook

Antonia Clare and JJ Wilson

Series Consultants
María Victoria Saumell and Sarah Louisa Birchley

ALWAYS LEARNING

PEARSON

ENGLISH in Common 4

with ActiveBook

Maria Victoria Saumell
Sarah Louisa Birchley

ALWAYS LEARNING

PEARSON

English in Common is a six-level course that helps adult and young-adult English learners develop effective communication skills that correspond to the Common European Framework of Reference for Languages (CEFR). Every level of *English in Common* is correlated to a level of the CEFR, and each lesson is formulated around a specific CAN DO objective.

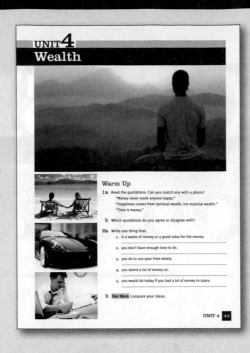

UNIT 4 — Wealth

Warm Up

1a Read the quotations. Can you match any with a photo?
"Money never made anyone happy."
"Happiness comes from spiritual wealth, not material wealth."
"Time is money."

b Which quotations do you agree or disagree with?

2a Write one thing that:
1. is a waste of money or a good value for the money.
2. you don't have enough time to do.
3. you do to use your time wisely.
4. you spend a lot of money on.
5. you would do today if you had a lot of money to spare.

b **Pair Work** Compare your ideas.

UNIT 4

English in Common 4 has ten units. Each unit has twelve pages.

There are three three-page lessons in each unit.

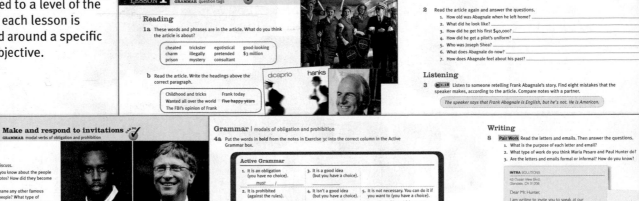

LESSON 1 — Make small talk — CAN DO
GRAMMAR question tags

Reading

1a These words and phrases are in the article. What do you think the article is about?

cheated	trickster	egotistical	good-looking
charm	illegally	pretended	$3 million
prison	mystery	consultant	

b Read the article. Write the headings above the correct paragraph.

Childhood and tricks — Frank today
Wanted all over the world — Five happy years
The FBI's opinion of Frank

dicaprio — hanks

2 Read the article again and answer the questions.
1. How old was Abagnale when he left home?
2. What did he look like?
3. How did he get his first $40,000?
4. How did he get a pilot's uniform?
5. Who was Joseph Shea?
6. What does Abagnale do now?
7. How does Abagnale feel about his past?

Listening

3 Listen to someone retelling Frank Abagnale's story. Find eight mistakes that the speaker makes, according to the article. Compare notes with a partner.

The speaker says that Frank Abagnale is English, but he's not. He is American.

LESSON 2 — Make and respond to invitations — CAN DO
GRAMMAR modal verbs of obligation and prohibition

Speaking

1 **Group Work** Discuss.
1. What do you know about the people in the photos? How did they become rich?
2. Can you name any other famous wealthy people? What type of reputation do they have? Do people like and admire them?

Sean "Puffy" Combs — Bill Gates

Vocabulary | personal qualities

2a **Pair Work** Check that you understand the expressions in the box.

be good with numbers	be confident	be ambitious
be good with people	be extravagant	be cheap
work long hours	be tolerant	be generous

Estée Lauder

b Discuss.
1. For which jobs do you need the qualities in the box?
An actor needs to be confident.
2. What qualities and habits do you think are necessary to be a successful entrepreneur?
3. Which qualities do you think you have?

entrepreneur n. someone who starts a company and arranges business deals

Listening

3a Listen to the first pa... Who is the seminar for? What is the topic?

b Listen to the rest of ... the expressions in Exercise ... mentions.

c Listen again and complete th...

d **Pair Work** Discuss.
1. Do you agree with the ... seminar? Explain your a...
2. Do you think you would ... entrepreneur? Why or w...

Grammar | modals of obligation and prohibition

4a Put the words in **bold** from the notes in Exercise 3c into the correct column in the Active Grammar box.

Active Grammar

1. It is an obligation (you have no choice).
   must?
2. It is prohibited (against the rules).
   must not
3. It is a good idea (but you have a choice).
4. It isn't a good idea (but you have a choice).
5. It is not necessary. You can do it if you want to (you have a choice).
   don't (doesn't) have to

See Reference page 130

b Read the sentences below. In which sentence do you have a choice? ___ In which sentence is something prohibited? ___
a. You can't smoke on an airplane.   b. You don't have to eat the food on an airplane.

5 Complete the sentences with modals.
Ex: Vivian has a bad headache. She _should_ take a pain reliever.
1. We _____ wear a suit to work. Dress pants and a shirt with a collar are fine.
2. You _____ buy your new computer now. There is going to be a big sale next week. You _____ wait until it goes on sale.
3. You _____ show your company ID card to the security guards at the reception desk. You _____ enter the building without it.
4. This is a smoke-free hotel. Guests _____ smoke in their rooms. They _____ go outside the building to smoke.

Writing

8 **Pair Work** Read the letters and emails. Then answer the questions.
1. What is the purpose of each letter and email?
2. What type of work do you think Maria Pesaro and Paul Hunter do?
3. Are the letters and emails formal or informal? How do you know?

INTRA SOLUTIONS
43 Ocean View Blvd.
Glendale, CA 91208

Dear Mr. Hunter,
I am writing to invite you to speak at our conference, *Entrepreneurs for the New Millennium*. Our company, Intra Solutions, helps young businessmen and businesswomen to develop their plans for the future.
The conference will take place at The Great Hall, 15 Grand Street, Los Angeles, CA, on Friday, July 14. We would like you to speak for one hour. I have enclosed the conference schedule and our brochure.
We look forward to hearing from you.
Yours sincerely,
Maria Pesaro
Maria Pesaro

Dear Ms. Pesaro,
Thank you for the ... your conference, ... *Millennium*. I will ... on the 14th. Coul... information about ... and equipment av... confirmation of ex...
Yours sincerely,
Paul Hunter

9a Write a letter inviting a famous person to give a talk at your school. Answ... Use the How To box and Maria's letter in Exercise 8 for ideas.
1. Who will you choose? Why?

LESSON 3 — Write a short classified ad — CAN DO
GRAMMAR factual conditional with *if/when/unless/as soon as*

Reading

1 Look at the two ads. What products are being advertised? How do the ads make you feel? Do they make you want to buy the products?

2a Discuss.
1. Do you think people spend more because of ads?
2. How do supermarkets and salespeople make us spend more?

b SPEAKING EXCHANGE Read the articles to find the answers.
Student A: Read about ads on this page.
Student B: Read about supermarkets on page 139.
Student C: Read about salespeople on page 141.

KOBE GETS HIS VITAMINS

How ads persuade you to spend more

Ads focus on either what products do or how the products make us feel. Our emotional response to a product is very important. If the ad makes us ...

Humor is also used, as funny ads are remembered longer. In addition, ad makers appeal to our senses. Unless your mouth waters, a chocolate ad is ...

3a SPEAKING EXCHANGE Now work in groups of three (one Student A, one Student B, and one Student C). Work together to complete the sentences.

Did you know . . . ?
1. Supermarkets often _____ to help us relax.
2. Supermarkets became very successful after introducing _____ in the 1940s.
3. Ads which use _____ are 10% more effective.
4. Ads are more memorable if they are _____.
5. Good salespeople can sell _____, to _____, at _____.
6. Salespeople may try to "mirror" the _____ of a buyer.

b Does any of the information surprise you?

Vocabulary | opposites

4a Write the opposites using the words in the box.

| punishment | sell | success | fail | consumer | reward | buyer | produce |

Verbs
1. Ex: succeed/ _fail_
2. buy/_____
3. _____/consume (a product)

Nouns
4. _____/failure
5. reward/_____
6. producer/_____

b Complete each sentence with a word from Exercise 4a.
1. Well done. You can have a _____ for passing your tests.
2. Teachers sometimes _____ students by giving them extra work to do.
3. The new advertising campaign was a complete _____. Sales have been terrible.
4. His first book was a great _____. It sold over a million copies.
5. Starting a business isn't easy. It is estimated that 40% of new businesses _____ within three years.

Pronunciation | word stress

5a Listen to the pairs of words from Exercise 4a and mark the main stress.

Grammar | factual conditional

7 Read the example sentences (1–6) ... choices to complete the rules (a–e...

Active Grammar
1. *If customers think of a se...*
2. *If I buy a lot now, I won't...*
3. *Supermarkets will usual...*
4. *As soon as you walk into...*
5. *Unless you buy this (face...*
6. *I will call you unless it is...*

Rules
For general present events,
Ex: *If an ad is good, you ...*
Ex: *When an ad is good, ...*
a. Use *if* + simple present + ...
b. Use *if/when* for events ...
c. Use *if/when* for events ...
d. Use *as soon as/unless* ...
e. *Unless* + positive verb m...

See Reference page 130

8 Complete the sentences using the ...
1. _____ (buy) a ne...
2. When I _____ (can) affo... (tell) him.
3. If you _____ (not ...(pay) a late...
4. I'm sure he _____ (be) somet...

A Unit Wrap Up ends each unit.

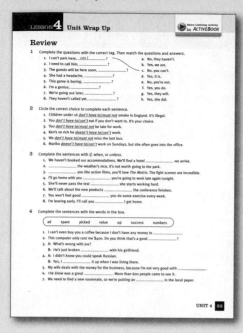
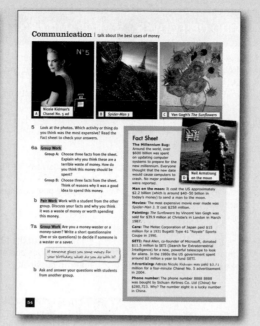

Back of Student Book

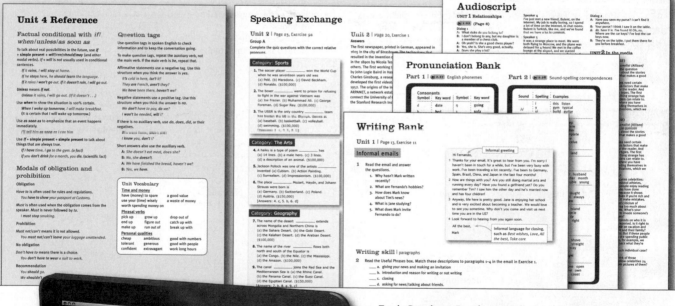

- Each Student Book contains an *ActiveBook*, which provides the Student Book in digital format. *ActiveBook* also includes the complete Audio Program and Extra Listening activities.

- An optional online **MyEnglishLab** provides the opportunity for extra practice anytime, anywhere.

- The Teacher's Resource Book contains teaching notes, photocopiable extension activities, and an *ActiveTeach*, which provides a digital Student Book enhanced by interactive whiteboard software. *ActiveTeach* also includes the videos and video activities, as well as the complete Test Bank.

Contents

READING/WRITING	LISTENING	COMMUNICATION/ PRONUNCIATION
Reading texts: • two articles about male and female statistics • an article about the pros and cons of Facebook • an article about the invention of the athletic shoe **Writing tasks:** • write a paragraph describing your relationship with a friend • write an email introducing yourself to a classmate	**Listening tasks:** • identify questions and answers • discern details • identify key phrases • match dialogs to photos	**Communication:** describe your friends and what you have in common **Pronunciation:** present perfect: *have/haven't*
Reading texts: • an article about the growth of mass media • two articles about quiz show scandals • news stories about strange events **Writing task:** write a short paragraph about a life event	**Listening tasks:** • understand the gist • determine the order of topics • discern details • confirm information	**Communication:** debate the value of news stories **Pronunciation:** past tense *-ed* endings
Reading texts: • property rental listings • an article about the world's greatest cities • an article about new cell phone technology **Writing task:** write a letter of complaint	**Listening tasks:** • identify key information/problems • recognize key words • confirm a prediction • understand key information in a telephone call	**Communication:** describe your dream house **Pronunciation:** compound nouns: stress
Reading texts: • an article about a famous thief and trickster • letters and emails • three articles about sales techniques **Writing task:** write and respond to an invitation	**Listening tasks:** • identify incorrect information • confirm information • understand the gist • recognize key expressions	**Communication:** talk about the best uses of money **Pronunciation:** • reduction of sounds • word stress
Reading texts: • an article about ways to become more creative • a bar graph illustrating a person's free time • an article about a strange travel experience **Writing task:** write a summary	**Listening tasks:** • understand/discern the gist • identify the speaker • determine important details • recognize key expressions	**Communication:** talk about something you are good at **Pronunciation:** vowels /æ/, /ɛ/, and /ɑ/
Reading texts: • an excerpt from a travel memoir • travel guides to Buenos Aires and Bangkok **Writing task:** write a travel guide for a city you know well	**Listening tasks:** • discern details/the gist • recognize key expressions • identify setting • identify key words	**Communication:** plan a trip using a travel guide **Pronunciation:** • intonation: questions • intonation: interest and surprise
Reading texts: • an article about accidental inventions • an essay about a childhood memory • profiles of remarkable senior citizens **Writing task:** write about a favorite teacher	**Listening tasks:** • match speakers with pictures • determine important details • confirm information	**Communication:** tell stories from your childhood **Pronunciation:** • *used to/didn't use to* • negative modals
Reading texts: • an article about changes in New York City • an article about the Live 8/Live Aid charity concerts **Writing tasks:** • write a newspaper article about an important issue • write about an important turning point in your life	**Listening tasks:** • match speakers with subjects • discern the gist • recognize key expressions • identify main idea	**Communication:** discuss your feelings about change **Pronunciation:** sentence rhythm
Reading texts: • an article about an unusual company • a humorous story about two types of workers • interviews about unusual jobs **Writing task:** write a company profile	**Listening tasks:** • determine important details • discern the gist • distinguish true and false information	**Communication:** prepare for a job interview
Reading texts: • three stories about memory • an article about wish-making beliefs • articles about Coco Chanel and Gianni Versace • two articles about types of goodbyes **Writing tasks:** • write endings for three stories • write a thank you letter	**Listening tasks:** • determine important details • identify key words • understand the gist • discern details	**Communication:** talk about your memories **Pronunciation:** numbers

Pronunciation Bank . . . page 150   Irregular Verbs . . . page 151   Audioscript . . . page 152   *ActiveBook* . . . Inside back cover

How much do you know . . . ?

1a Do you know these tenses? Match the sentences (1–7) to the tenses (a–g).

_____ 1. I've lived here since I was a child.

_____ 2. She's studying Spanish in Mexico.

_____ 3. We left the office at about 7:00 P.M.

_____ 4. I'd already eaten lunch, so I wasn't hungry.

_____ 5. He was playing his guitar when the string broke.

_____ 6. I'm leaving the company in July.

_____ 7. I write about fifteen emails a day.

a. **simple present**

b. **present continuous** (for ongoing actions)

c. **present continuous** (for future actions)

d. **present perfect**

e. **simple past**

f. **past continuous**

g. **past perfect**

b Complete the sentences by writing the name of the correct tense from Exercise 1a.

1. Use the _____ to describe something that started and finished in the past.

2. Use the _____ to describe a future plan.

3. Use the _____ to describe something that started in the past and continues in the present.

4. Use the _____ to describe something that is a state, habit, or general truth.

5. Use the _____ to describe a temporary situation that is happening around now.

6. Use the _____ to describe something that happened before another event in the past.

7. Use the _____ to describe something temporary that was in progress at a time in the past.

2 Label the underlined parts of the sentences using the headings in the box.

> prefix   suffix   phrasal verb   idiom

_____ 1. The story was <u>un</u>believable!

_____ 2. Can you <u>give me a hand</u> with this?

_____ 3. She <u>grew up</u> in Ecuador.

_____ 4. I've <u>given up</u> eating chocolate!

_____ 5. This meat is <u>over</u>cooked.

_____ 6. Happ<u>iness</u> is the most important thing.

_____ 7. This is the poem that I <u>learned by heart</u>.

_____ 8. This old computer is use<u>less</u>.

3a Complete the chart with the correct verbs, nouns, and adjectives.

verb	noun	adjective
educate	(1.) _____	_educated_
(2.) _____	_improvement_	_improved_
xxx	_expense_	(3.) _____
xxx	_beauty_	(4.) _____
attract	_attraction_	(5.) _____

b Mark the main stress in the words above. How many syllables are there?

4 Write the words in the correct order to make useful phrases for the classroom.

1. could/a/little,/speak/you/please/up/? _____

2. dictionary/I/could/your/borrow/? _____

3. in/do/English/say/you/how/"XXX"/? _____

4. mean/does/"XXX"/what/? _____

5. and/the/between/what's/"X"/"Y"/difference/? _____

6. you/again/say/can/that/? _____

UNIT **1**
Relationships

A

B

C

D

Warm Up

1 Look at the photos. What types of relationships do they show?

2 **Pair Work** Put the words and phrases in the box in groups: **a.** work/school, **b.** family, **c.** friends, **d.** other. Can you add any more words to each category?

husband	close friend	teammate	acquaintance	boss
co-worker	best friend	stepmother	ex-girlfriend	stranger
old friend	classmate	father-in-law	friend of a friend	

3 **Pair Work** Think of four people you know. Tell your partner about them. Describe your relationship.

> *My best friend's name is Maria . . .*

Make generalizations

GRAMMAR auxiliary verbs

Vocabulary | collocations

1a Complete the questions using the prepositions in the box.

> about   on   in   for   to   at

1. What activities and hobbies are you **good** _____?
2. What do you **use** the Internet _____?
3. What do you **spend** most of your money _____?
4. What do you **worry** _____?
5. What types of exercise are you **crazy** _____?
6. What do you usually **talk** _____ with friends?
7. What cultures are you **interested** _____?
8. What clubs do you **belong** _____?

b **Pair Work** Choose five of the questions to ask other students.

Listening

2 ▶1.02 Listen to the dialogs. Which questions from Exercise 1a do the speakers answer? Complete the chart. Then listen again. Can you add any more information about what the speakers said?

	Question?	Answer?	More information
Dialog 1	8	chess club	very good, plays every day
Dialog 2			
Dialog 3			

Grammar | auxiliary verbs

3 Complete the Active Grammar box with sentences from the dialog below.

A: I'm crazy about running.

B: **Do** you do it regularly?

A: Yes, I **do**. Three or four t imes a week.

B: Where **do** you run?

A: In the park. I **don't** run very fast.

Active Grammar

Yes/No questions

Begin with *do/does* in the present, *did* in the past, and *have/has* in the present perfect. The order is auxiliary + subject + verb.

1. Ex: _____

Wh- questions

The question word comes before the auxiliary. The order is question word + auxiliary + subject + verb.

2. Ex: _____

Short answers

Use the auxiliary verb from the question.

3. Ex: _____

Negative statements

Use *don't/doesn't* in the present, *didn't* in the past, and *haven't/hasn't* in the present perfect.

4. Ex: _____

See Reference page 127

4 Complete the dialogs. Write questions using the words in parentheses.

Ex: A: (what) _What's your favorite color?_   B: Blue.

1. A: (what) _____ B: Swimming.
2. A: (who) _____ B: With my parents.
3. A: (do) _____ B: Yes, I do. He's my favorite actor.
4. A: (have) _____ B: No, I haven't. Is it good?
5. A: (when) _____ B: At ten o'clock.

Speaking

5a Complete the chart. Think of four things that your classmates don't know about you. Write one or two words.

family:	
free time:	
likes/dislikes:	
spending money:	

b **Pair Work** Look at your partner's chart. Ask questions to get more information.

> Do you live with your parents?

> No, I don't. I live with my sister.

Reading

6a Do you think these sentences are true (*T*) or false (*F*)?

____ 1. Men live longer than women.

____ 2. Most men are happy with their weight.

____ 3. Women watch more TV than men.

____ 4. Sixty-five percent of men do some physical exercise.

____ 5. Men like to talk about relationships.

b **Pair Work** **Student A:** Read article A. Find the answers to 1–2. **Student B:** Read article B on page 10. Find the answers to 3–5. Tell your partner which sentences are true, according to the article.

Article A
Health and wealth

Life, love, and death

In the developed world, the average man lives until he is 75.4 years old, and the average woman lives to 80.2. In general, the illness that causes the most deaths is heart disease, and Monday is the most common day for a heart attack. Men tend not to get married until they are 30, but the average woman marries at 28. Men admit to causing a serious argument with their spouse seven times a year, but women claim they are only guilty of this once a year. Thirty percent of men buy flowers for their partners after an argument.

Work, habits, and body

A recent study of 63 countries shows that women who work full time earn 16% less than men who work full time. Globally, 48% of men and 12% of women smoke. While all smokers say that they smoke to reduce stress and be social, women are more likely to smoke in order to lose weight. The average person in the developed world will eat 27,200 kilograms (59,840 pounds) of food in his or her lifetime—the weight of more than six elephants. Men eat more meat and poultry, especially duck, veal, and ham. Women generally eat more vegetables, especially carrots and tomatoes. But strangely enough, men eat more asparagus and brussels sprouts! And only 36% of men worry about their weight. On the other hand, 90% of women don't like their bodies and the average woman tries to diet six times in her life.

Article B
Free time and chat

Leisure activities

Men and women are nearly equal in the living room. In the developed world, women watch TV or listen to the radio for 2 hours and 37 minutes a day, only 20 minutes less than men. On the other hand, women are in the kitchen, or doing the housework, for 2 hours and 18 minutes, while men spend just 45 minutes doing housework. For exercise, women go to the gym or do yoga. Men go for a walk or, in 35% of cases, don't do anything at all. Men like driving more than women, though 95% of drivers of both sexes consider themselves to be "above average" drivers.

Conversation topics

Regarding chat, women tend to talk a lot about relationships and other people, and they say about 7,000 words a day. Men talk about sports and use only 2,000 words a day. Men's conversations that aren't about sports tend to be about work, politics, economics, or abstract ideas, for example "the meaning of life."

7a What do these numbers refer to in the articles? Write sentences and use your own words.

| 75.4 | 80.2 | 90% | 35% | 2 hours and 18 minutes | 7,000 |

> On average, men in the developed world live to 75.4 years.

b **Group Work** Discuss. Which facts did you find surprising? In what ways do you think you are like the average man or woman? Refer to the articles.

Speaking

8a Look at the How To box. Check the expressions that are in the articles.

How To:

Make generalizations	
Talk about averages	_____ The average (man/woman) . . .
	_____ On average, . . .
Make generalizations	_____ In general, . . . / . . . in general . . .
	_____ Generally, . . . / . . . generally . . .
	_____ Usually, . . . / . . . usually . . .
Talk about tendencies	_____ (Women) tend to (talk a lot about) . . .
	_____ (Men) don't tend to (do housework).
	_____ (Men) tend not to (get married until age 30).

b **Group Work** Look at the list of topics below. Make as many generalizations as you can in five minutes. Use expressions from the How To box.

men	big cities	non-smokers	small towns
women	smokers	poor countries	rich countries

> *Women tend to have fewer car accidents than men.*   > *In general, men enjoy driving.*

Speaking

1a **Pair Work** Read these quotes about friendship. Which ones do you agree with? Compare your ideas.

> "To like and dislike the same things: that is a true friendship."

> "I have never had better friends than the ones I had when I was 12."

> "Strangers are just friends waiting to happen."

> "A real friend is one who walks in when the rest of the world walks out."

b Complete the sentence with your ideas. Read your sentence to the class.

A real friend is . . .

Vocabulary | friendship

2 Match the phrases in **bold** with the definitions.

Phrase	Definition
____ 1. Let's **keep in touch**.	a. not stay in contact
____ 2. We **have the same sense of humor**.	b. like to be with him or her
____ 3. We **have a lot in common**.	c. know him or her better
____ 4. I hope we don't **lose touch**.	d. find the same things funny
____ 5. He's really nice when you **get to know him**.	e. like or enjoy the same things
____ 6. I really **enjoy her company**.	f. have a friendly relationship
____ 7. We **get along** really well.	g. stay in contact

Listening

3a ▶1.03 Listen to five people talk about a friend. Which speaker met his or her friend:

____ 1. by using a computer?   ____ 3. in a parking lot?   ____ 5. while studying?

____ 2. at an office?   ____ 4. in an airport?

b Listen again. Complete each speaker's words.

Speaker 1: . . . we _____ for a while . . .

Speaker 2: We have the same _____ of _____ . . .

Speaker 3: . . . and I really enjoy _____.

Speaker 4: . . . we've found that we have a lot _____.

Speaker 5: After that trip, we just _____ in _____.

4 **Pair Work** Discuss. Where do you go to meet new friends? How did you meet your closest friend?

Reading

5 What do you know about Facebook? Are you a member of any social networking websites? Why or why not?

6 Read the article. Then answer the questions.

639 of your closest friends— the pros and cons of Facebook

Monica Harper is sitting alone in a café. But she's not completely alone—one click on her smart phone connected her with her 639 Facebook friends. She has already chatted with one person, viewed her cousin Sara's wedding pictures, and sent two birthday e-cards. Now she is scanning the status updates and learns that her boyfriend just got the job he interviewed for. Wait, why didn't he call her first? Never mind. He got the job!

Like many of her friends, Monica has been using Facebook for several years. With over 500 million members worldwide and growing rapidly, Facebook is a social networking phenomenon. Half of Facebook members log on daily. Many like Monica check in numerous times a day. "When my workplace blocked Facebook access, I just set up my smart phone to receive updates," she says. "I like to know what's going on with everyone. Facebook makes this very easy."

Daniel Modeski is less enthusiastic. "Actually, I'm considering quitting Facebook," he admits. "I joined to stay connected with my family after going away to college. But it's a huge distraction. You log on thinking you're just going to check your messages and, before you know it, you're writing status updates, watching videos, and playing games. There's always something to do," Daniel explains. "And that's not a good thing when I have an exam the next day."

A bigger drawback for Daniel is privacy. "I post messages and photos for people I know. But I feel like strangers are looking at my stuff." Problems with Facebook's privacy controls have caused users to worry that their personal information may not be private. "I'm very careful about what I post," says Daniel. "If I deleted my account, I wouldn't have to worry. But I'd probably lose touch with a lot of people."

Monica would never quit Facebook, but she admits she sometimes needs a break. "I can get a little obsessed, wondering why no one replied to my post or commented on my photos. Last month an old college roommate didn't accept my friend request. I was shocked and hurt," Monica recalls.

For good or bad, it appears that social networking sites are here to stay. They keep us connected and give us a sense of belonging. But it's important to remember that the social circle they create is virtual. In the real world, it would be impossible to keep up with 639 friends! So yes, definitely interact on Facebook. But then take a step back. Go have lunch with a live person. And before you sit down, log off. You can update your status later!

1. Does Monica enjoy using Facebook? _____
2. What social networking activities does Monica do? _____
3. How often does Monica log on? _____
4. Why did Daniel join Facebook? _____
5. Why does Daniel want to quit? _____
6. What disadvantage of Facebook does Monica mention? _____
7. What advice does the article give to Facebook users? _____

7 **Pair Work** Discuss.

1. Do you think it is easy to stay connected with friends and family? Why or why not?
2. Do you worry about posting personal information online? What can you do to protect your privacy?

Grammar | simple present and present continuous

8a Look at the sentences (1–5) below. Match the rules (a–e) in the Active Grammar box to the sentences. Write the letter on the line.

_____ 1. We **are** both **taking** photography courses this semester.

_____ 2. She **is expecting** a message.

_____ 3. Louise and Juanita **write** every day.

_____ 4. She **lives** in Vancouver.

_____ 5. There **are** many dangers.

b What is the difference in meaning between these two sentences?

1. What **do** you **think** about our new teacher?

2. What **are** you **thinking** about?

> ### Active Grammar
>
> 1. Use the **simple present** for:
>   a. habits/routines.
>   b. things that are always true/permanent.
>   c. describing a state/situation.
> 2. Use the **present continuous** for:
>   d. things that are happening now at this precise moment.
>   e. temporary situations that are happening around now.
>
> Some verbs are not usually used in the continuous form: *hate, want, need.*

See Reference page 127

9 Put the verbs into the correct form of the simple present or present continuous.

1. _____ (you/read) that book? Can I see it?

2. Sasha _____ (not work) on Tuesdays, so she's at home now.

3. I'm so tired. I _____ (need) a vacation!

4. That looks hard. _____ (you/want) any help?

5. Where _____ (you/live) these days?

6. _____ (you/understand) this computer manual?

7. I _____ (not/want) to leave too late because I _____ (hate) driving at night.

8. What horrible weather! I _____ (stay) inside until the rain stops.

10a Write questions using the cues and the simple present or present continuous.

1. What/you/do? (job/occupation) _____

2. What/you/do/at work (or school)/these days? _____

3. How often/you/go out with friends? _____

4. What/you/like/do? _____

5. What movies/you/like/watch? _____

6. What/you/usually/do/on the weekends? _____

7. you/read/a good book/at the moment? _____

8. you/play (or watch)/any sports/these days? _____

9. Why/you/study/English/this year? _____

10. you/take/any other courses/this semester? _____

b **Pair Work** Ask your partner the questions in Exercise 10a. Then tell the class anything interesting you learned.

Writing

11 Read the email and complete the exercises in the Writing Bank on page 144. Write an email introducing yourself to a new classmate.

Retell a simple narrative in your own words

GRAMMAR present perfect and simple past; *for* and *since*

Listening

1a ▶1.04 Listen to three people talking about someone who they had an argument with. Match the speakers to the photos. Write the number of the speaker in the box.

A ☐   B ☐   C ☐

b [Pair Work] Listen again and complete the chart. Then check your answers with a partner.

	Speaker 1	Speaker 2	Speaker 3
Who does the speaker talk about?	*Romina—best friend*		
How long have they known/did they know each other?			
Why/When did they argue?			
How is their relationship now?			

2 [Pair Work] Discuss. Have you ever argued with a close friend or family member? What happened? What do friends or families usually argue about?

Reading

3a You are going to read about two famous inventors. Look at the pictures. What do you think the story is about?

A ☐

C ☐

B ☐

D ☐

3b Read the article. Then look at the pictures in Exercise 3a again. Number the pictures (1–4) in the correct order.

Brotherly Love?

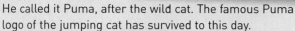
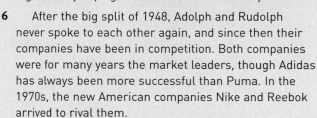

Adidas and Puma have been two of the biggest names in athletic shoe manufacturing for over half a century.

1 Since 1928 they have supplied shoes for Olympic athletes, World Cup-winning football heroes, Muhammad Ali, hip hop stars, and famous rock musicians all over the world. But the story of these two companies begins in one house in the town of Herzogenaurach, Germany.

2 Adolph and Rudolph Dassler were the sons of a shoemaker. They loved sports but complained that they could never find comfortable shoes to play in. Rudolph always said, "You cannot play sports wearing shoes that you'd walk around town with." So they started making their own. In 1920 Adolph made the first pair of athletic shoes with cleats,[1] produced on the Dasslers' kitchen table.

3 On July 1, 1924, they formed a shoe company, Dassler Brothers Ltd. The company became successful and it provided the shoes for Germany's athletes at the 1928 and 1932 Olympic Games.

4 But in 1948 the brothers argued. No one knows exactly what happened, but family members have suggested that the argument may have been about money. The result was that Adolph left the company. His nickname[2] was Adi, and using this and the first three letters of the family name, Dassler, he founded Adidas.

5 Rudolph relocated across the River Aurach and founded his own company, too. He called it Puma, after the wild cat. The famous Puma logo of the jumping cat has survived to this day.

6 After the big split of 1948, Adolph and Rudolph never spoke to each other again, and since then their companies have been in competition. Both companies were for many years the market leaders, though Adidas has always been more successful than Puma. In the 1970s, the new American companies Nike and Reebok arrived to rival them.

7 The terrible family argument should really be forgotten, but ever since it happened, over 50 years ago, the town has been split into two. Even now, some Adidas employees and Puma employees don't talk to each other.

> **Glossary**
> [1] *cleats* = short pieces of rubber or metal on the bottom of a shoe
> [2] *nickname* = name (not your real name) given to you by friends and family

4 Mark the sentences true (*T*) or false (*F*), according to the article.

_____ 1. The Dasslers' father was an Olympic athlete.

_____ 2. The brothers first made athletic shoes at home.

_____ 3. They argued about the shoes.

_____ 4. Adolph and Rudolph decided to start their own companies.

_____ 5. Puma sells more shoes than Adidas.

_____ 6. People in the town have now forgotten the argument.

5 Find verbs in the article which mean the following:

_____ 1. provided a product (paragraph 1)

_____ 2. created (an institution/company, etc.) (paragraph 4)

_____ 3. moved permanently to a different place (paragraph 5)

_____ 4. be in competition with another person or company (paragraph 6)

6 **Pair Work** Close your book and take turns retelling the Dassler brothers' story in your own words.

Grammar 1 | present perfect and simple past

7a Identify each underlined verb as the present perfect or the simple past.

1. *Since 1928 they <u>have supplied</u> shoes for Olympic athletes, . . .*
2. *On July 1, 1924, they <u>formed</u> a shoe company.*
3. *After the big split of 1948 . . . their companies <u>have been</u> in competition.*

b Read the Active Grammar box and circle the correct choices to complete the rules.

> ## Active Grammar
>
> 1. Use the <u>simple past</u>/<u>present perfect</u> to describe an action that started in the past and continues in the present.
> 2. Use the <u>simple past</u>/<u>present perfect</u> to talk about something that happened in the past but has a result in the present.
> 3. To describe something that happened at a specific time use the <u>simple past</u>/<u>present perfect</u>.

See Reference page 127

8 Complete the dialogs using the verbs in the box. Use the present perfect or the simple past.

> decide   lose   have   find   see   put

1. **A:** _I've decided_ to stop smoking.
   B: That's great! When _____ (1.) this?
   A: Last Monday. I _____ (2.) a cigarette for three days.
   B: Congratulations!
   A: I _____ (3.) a cigar yesterday, though.
   B: Oh.

2. **A:** _____ (4.) my purse? I can't find it anywhere.
   B: Your purse? I think I _____ (5.) it on the table.
   A: Ah, here it is. I _____ (6.) it! Oh, no. Where are the car keys? I _____ (7.) the car keys now.
   B: They're on the table. I _____ (8.) them there for you before breakfast.

Pronunciation | present perfect: *have/haven't*

9a ▶1.05 Listen to the dialogs in Exercise 8. How is *have* pronounced in:
a. positive sentences?   b. negative sentences?

b **Pair Work** Practice the dialogs.

Grammar 2 | *for* and *since*

10a Read the Active Grammar box and circle the correct choices to complete rules 1 and 2.

b Complete the sentences with *for* or *since*.

1. I've lived in the same house _____ I was born.
2. I've studied English _____ about 3 years.
3. I've been at this school _____ a few weeks.
4. I've had the same hobby _____ 30 years.
5. I've known my best friend _____ I started school.

> ## Active Grammar
>
> The present perfect is often used with *for* and *since*.
>
> *Puma has sold shoes **for** over 50 years.*
>
> *Adidas has sold shoes **since** 1948.*
>
> 1. Use *for* + <u>period of</u>/<u>point in</u> time
> 2. Use *since* + <u>period of</u>/<u>point in</u> time

See Reference page 127

c **Pair Work** Make each sentence in Exercise 10b true for you. Then take turns reading your sentences. Ask questions to get more information.

LESSON 4 **Unit Wrap Up**

Extra Vocabulary Study and
Extra Listening Activity
in *ACTIVEBOOK*

Review

1   Circle the correct auxiliary verb.

   Ex: Mary (is)/has taking a shower.

   1. They *are/do* writing in their journals now.
   2. *Had/Have* your friends spoken to you today?
   3. I *don't/haven't* understand this question.
   4. *Do/Are* we going to a concert tonight?
   5. She *has/is* never been to Hawaii before.
   6. *Doesn't/Don't* his mother live here?
   7. *Haven't/Didn't* we seen this movie already?
   8. *Does/Has* Mr. Hernandez arrived yet?

2   Complete the dialogs using auxiliary verbs.

   1. A: Hi. _Do_ you know many people here?
      B: Yes, a few. Some of us _____ taking an English course together.
   2. A: _____ you staying in a nice hotel?
      B: Actually, we _____ like it very much.
   3. A: _____ you know this area well?
      B: No, we _____. We _____ never been here before.
   4. A: _____ you like the city?
      B: Yes, we _____ enjoying our stay here.
   5. A: _____ you worked here long?
      B: No, I _____. Only one year.
   6. A: Liz! What _____ you doing here in Rio?!
      B: I _____ traveling around South America!
   7. A: _____ we met before?
      B: Yes, we _____. We met in Jakarta.

3   Complete the sentences using the cues and the simple present or the present continuous.

   Ex: I'm _going out_ (go out) now. I'll see you later.

   1. We can take a walk. It _____ (not/rain) now.
   2. Alexis _____ (have) two older brothers. They look just like him!
   3. Olga _____ (stay) at the Palace Hotel. She checked in last night.
   4. Our grandmother is in the hospital. We _____ (want) to visit her as soon as possible.
   5. Is it five o'clock already? I _____ (not believe) it. I feel like I just got here!
   6. Al is busy. He _____ (work) on a new project that has to be finished by Friday.

4   Complete the sentences using the cues and the simple past or the present perfect.

   Ex: We _worked_ (work) hard last night.

   1. I _____ (not call) her yesterday because I was busy.
   2. _____ (you ever eat) Thai food? It's delicious.
   3. Technology _____ (influence) the way we live now.
   4. He _____ (stop) running when he got tired.
   5. We _____ (not see) each other since April.
   6. Who is Jo? I _____ (never hear) of her.
   7. They _____ (wake up) at 7:00 A.M. this morning.

5   Complete the sentences with words or phrases that mean the same as the words in parentheses.

   Ex: Let me introduce you to my _co-worker_ Gonzalo. (someone you work with)

   1. He was a complete _____. (someone you don't know)
   2. We get along well because we _____ common. (share similar interests)
   3. I haven't seen Ali in class for a couple of months. I'm _____ him. (afraid something may be wrong)
   4. We're staying in their house for a whole month. Luckily, we _____ really well. (have a friendly relationship)
   5. Mike didn't have a ride to his soccer game, but his _____ offered to pick him up. (member of his team)

UNIT 1   17

Communication | describe your friends and what you have in common

The tree of friends

6 Choose six friends and write their names in the boxes around the tree. Think about some of the following questions. Write notes.

  1. What was your first impression of each other?

  2. Why do you like him or her?

  3. What things do you have in common?

  4. What type of character does he or she have?

  5. How do you keep in touch?

  6. What job does he or she do?

  7. What activities or hobbies is he or she crazy about?

7a **Pair Work** Describe your friends to your partner. Talk about how you met and what you have in common.

b Find out which of your partner's friends would get along with your friends. Find five things they have in common.

8 Write a paragraph describing your relationship with one of your friends from Exercise 6. Use the questions and your notes to help you. Think about how you met and how your relationship has developed.

UNIT 2
In the media

Warm Up

1a Read the paragraph about changes in the media.

> The media—all of the organizations that provide news and information—is changing rapidly. Until recently, most people kept informed about the events happening around them by watching **TV** or reading **newspapers, books,** and **magazines**. However, advances in technology have created new ways of getting information. Book publishers now sell more downloads of **digital e-books** than hardcover books. Fewer people are subscribing to newspapers and magazines—they're going online to use **news websites, blogs, video-sharing websites, message boards,** and **social networking sites**.

b Which of the types of media in **bold** can you find in the photos?

2 **Group Work** Discuss.

1. Which types of media do you use most and least often? Explain why.
2. Do you think that printed media like books and magazines will disappear and be replaced by electronic media like e-books and websites? Why or why not?

Give opinions and agree/disagree

CAN DO ✓

GRAMMAR the passive voice

Reading

1 **Pair Work** Discuss. In what order were these items invented? (See page 137 for answers.) Which have been the most important?

> TV   newspapers   the Internet   radio   video

2a How much do you know about the media? Answer the questions.

1. What is the world's most popular TV show?
2. Which country makes the most movies?
3. Which search engine is the most popular?
4. Which movie is often voted the greatest ever?
5. Which country has the most Internet users?
6. Which country watches the most TV?
7. Which newspaper sells the most copies?

b Read the article to check your answers.

Who watches the most TV?

ON TOP OF THE MEDIA

Who makes the most movies?

"The mass media is a combination of information, entertainment and complete rubbish." *D. Yandell*

You may or may not agree with psychologist David Yandell, but most people agree that the media has one key characteristic: It keeps growing and growing. These days, few people can remember life before television. And most of us have been influenced by the constant flow of words and images from screens or newspapers. Some of it is certainly garbage, and some of it is wonderful. Here are some of the "firsts" and "bests" of the media world.

The #1 search engine: Google. A lot of information can be found by searching Google. In fact, it is used for over 250 million searches in 182 languages every day. It was named after googol, which is the number represented by one followed by 100 zeros.

The #1 movie industry: The Indian movie industry (nicknamed Bollywood). More movies are made in India than in any other country.

The #1 selling newspaper: *Yomiuri Shimbun*. It sells 10 million copies a day in Japan.

The #1 Internet user: Iceland has the highest percentage of population using the Internet. Of a population of 308,910, at least 301,600 use the Internet—97.6% of the population.

The #1 TV show: *China's Got Talent*. With everything from break-dancing street cleaners to an armless pianist, this talent show has an audience of over 500 million viewers!

The #1 country of TV addicts: The US has 805 televisions per 1,000 people, the world's highest number, and in the US people also watch TV the most. By the age of 65 the average US citizen has spent nine years in front of the TV.

The #1 movie: *Citizen Kane*. In lists of great movies, it usually comes first. It was directed by Orson Welles in 1941 and tells the story of a media tycoon.*

Citizen Kane

Glossary
* *media tycoon* = a person who owns newspapers, TV stations, etc. People like this are rich and powerful.

3a Read the article again and mark the sentences true (*T*), false (*F*), or no information (*NI*).

_____ 1. According to the article, most people think the media contains a lot of garbage.

_____ 2. Googol is a number.

_____ 3. Orson Welles was a media tycoon.

_____ 4. Americans watch more TV than any other nationality.

_____ 5. *Yomiuri Shimbun* is a daily newspaper.

_____ 6. *China's Got Talent* is seen in over 50 countries.

American English	British English
garbage	rubbish

b Check any information in the article that you already knew. Write (!) if you were surprised by any information. Compare with a partner.

Grammar | the passive voice

4 Read the Active Grammar box and match the rules (1–3) to these sentences from the article.

_____ a. The TV was invented in 1926 by John Logie Baird.

_____ b. John Logie Baird invented the TV in 1926.

_____ c. The TV was invented in 1926.

5 Complete the sentences with the active or passive voice. Use the simple present or simple past.

1. A top politician _____ (remove) from office last week.

2. The CEO of HAW Steel _____ (give) $1 million bonus by company directors last month.

3. Parents _____ (advise) to limit children's TV viewing to ten hours per week.

4. The body of a famous climber _____ (find) in the Himalayan mountains in June.

5. Mario Vargas Llosa _____ (win) the Nobel Prize in Literature in 2010.

6. A new health report finds that fewer games _____ (play) at school than ever before.

Active Grammar

	Passive voice
simple present	*Many films **are made** in India.*
simple past	*Citizen Kane **was directed** by Orson Welles.*
present perfect	*Most of us **have been influenced** by TV.*
modal verbs	*A lot of information **can be found** by searching Google.*

1. Use the **active** voice to describe what someone or something does or has done.

2. Use the **passive** voice to describe what happens or has happened to someone or something (often when the person or thing that does the action is not known or not important.)

3. **By** is often used to say who or what does the action in a passive sentence.

See Reference page 128

Speaking

6a Complete the sentences to make them true for you.

1. The last present I was given was _____.

2. When I was younger I was told _____.

3. I have been helped by _____.

4. Recently I have been taught how to _____.

b Pair Work Say your sentences to other students. Add at least one piece of information to each sentence. Has anyone had similar experiences?

Listening

7a ▶1.06 Listen to the first part of an interview with a journalist. Is the journalist talking about:

    a. types of journalists?   **b.** types of stories?   **c.** types of newspapers?

b ▶1.07 Listen to the whole interview. The journalist talks about the topics below. Number them in the order she mentions them.

    ____ **a.** Writing about people's private lives

    ____ **b.** Celebrities who need publicity

    ____ **c.** Newspapers which write only about celebrities

    ____ **d.** Famous people who do something wrong

c Listen again. What does the journalist say about each topic? Write notes and then compare your answers with a partner.

Speaking

8a Complete the How To box with the headings below.

> Agreeing   Asking for an opinion
> Disagreeing   Giving an opinion

How To:	
Give opinions and (dis)agree	
a. _____	*I think . . .* *In my opinion . . .*
b. _____	*What do you think?* *What's your opinion?*
c. _____	*Definitely.* *Me, too. (to agree with I think . . .)* *Me neither. (to agree with I don't think . . .)*
d. _____	*I'm not sure about that.* *I don't think so.*

b ▶1.08 Listen to five speakers. Decide if you agree or disagree with each person's opinion.

Speaker	1	2	3	4	5
Agree					
Disagree					

c **Pair Work** Discuss your opinions with your partner. Use phrases from the How To box.

> *I agree. I think newspapers should be free.*

> *I'm not sure about that. Newspapers need money to pay their employees.*

Deal with problems

GRAMMAR relative clauses

CAN DO ✓

Listening

1a ▶1.09 Listen to four people talking about what can go wrong on a live TV show. Which speaker talks about each problem?

——— 1. technical problems

——— 2. reading bad news

——— 3. forgetting to take off the microphone

——— 4. problems with furniture

——— 5. people laughing

——— 6. people getting nervous

——— 7. problems with names of places

——— 8. people forgetting what to say

b Listen again to check your answers. What do the speakers say about each thing? Take notes and compare with a partner.

2 Read the How To box. Can you add any more phrases or expressions?

How To:	
Deal with problems	
Ask what the problem is	*What's the problem/matter?*
Explain the problem	*The copier is out of order/isn't working.*
	It is broken/keeps breaking (down).
	My boss keeps shouting at me.
Offer a solution	*I'll deal with it/fix it.*
	Should I call the office manager?
	Try turning it off.

3a Complete the dialogs with language from the How To box.

——— 1. **A:** What's the _____ (1.)?

   B: The printer's _____ (2.) again.

   A: Should I _____ (3.) the IT department?

——— 2. **A:** Oh no! My computer _____ (4.) freezing!

   B: _____ (5.) turning it off and on again.

   A: Thanks.

——— 3. **A:** What's the matter?

   B: The copier isn't _____ (6.). I think it's out of paper.

   A: Don't worry. I'll _____ (7.) it.

b ▶1.10 Listen and check your answers.

c **Pair Work** Practice the dialogs.

Speaking

4a Imagine you are having a bad day at work or school. Everything is going wrong. Write three problems that you are having.

1. _____
   _____

2. _____
   _____

3. _____
   _____

b **Pair Work** Role play dealing with the problems you wrote in Exercise 4a. Then change roles. Use language from the How To box on page 23.
Student A: Tell Student B about your problems.
Student B: Ask what Student A's problems are and offer solutions.

Reading

5a **Pair Work** **Student A:** Read the article below. **Student B:** Read the article on page 138 in the Speaking Exchange. Answer the questions.

1. What was the TV show?
2. Why was there a scandal?
3. Who was involved in the scandal?
4. What happened in the end?

b Tell your partner about your story. Use your notes to help you.

Who Wants to Be a Millionaire?

Since making its debut in September 1998, the game show *Who Wants to Be a Millionaire?* has become a worldwide hit. On September 10, 2001, Charles Ingram became one of the lucky (and intelligent) people who won the big prize—1.6 million dollars. So why, when he returned to the dressing room, did he have an argument with his wife? Why didn't he celebrate? It was because they cheated, and they were nervous about getting caught.

When the truth was revealed 19 months later, they were caught. During the show which Ingram won, viewers heard someone coughing regularly. It was a college professor friend of theirs, Tecwen Whittock. He was in the studio, and the moment when he heard the correct answer, he coughed. Ingram never admitted cheating, but viewers who saw the show said that the cheating was obvious. On some occasions Ingram actually changed his answer after coughs from Whittock told him he was wrong. A doctor later said that Whittock suffered from an allergy that was making him cough. But the 15.1 million people who watched a replay of the show on a later documentary had other ideas.

Charles, his wife, and his friend were all found guilty of cheating and ordered to return the prize money and to pay fines and legal fees totalling $186,000. Luckily for them, when they were sentenced, they were not sent to prison.

Grammar | relative clauses

6a Complete these sentences from the articles using the relative pronouns in the box.

> who   where   which
> when   whose   that

1. Ingram became one of the lucky people _____ won the big prize.

2. During the game _____ Ingram won, viewers heard someone coughing regularly.

3. He nervously looked around the studio _____ he was being filmed.

4. The man _____ fame meant that he received 500 letters a day was also a cheat.

5. Whittock suffered from an allergy _____ was making him cough.

6. The moment _____ he heard the correct answer, he coughed.

Active Grammar

*Ingram became one of the lucky people **who won the big prize** . . .*

"*. . . who won the big prize . . .*" is an example of a defining relative clause; it defines exactly who or what we are talking about. This is essential information about a person, a place, or a thing.

1. Use ___*who*___ or _____ for people.

2. Use _____ or _____ for things or animals.

3. Use _____ for places.

4. Use _____ for possessions.

5. Use _____ for time.

The pronouns *who*, *which*, or *that* can be left out if they are the object of the relative clause.

Game shows are programs I never watch.

See Reference page 128

b Use the words in Exercise 6a to complete the rules (1–5) in the Active Grammar box.

7 Add *who*, *which*, or *where* to each sentence, if necessary.

Ex: That's the TV studio ^*where* they film *China's Got Talent*.

1. That's the studio the last Guillermo del Toro film was made.

2. He's the man helps the director.

3. I've already seen the movies Matt rented.

4. The game show host is the same woman reads the news.

5. Did she like the camera you bought her?

6. Here's the house I grew up.

8 Link each pair of sentences by using *who*, *where*, *which*, *whose*, *when*, or *that*. There may be more than one possible answer.

Ex: That's the road. The accident happened there.

That's the road where the accident happened.

1. That's the man. He won the big prize.

2. This is her new novel. It has already sold 500,000 copies.

3. We work for a small company. You haven't heard of the company.

4. I like the start of spring. Flowers begin to grow.

5. We met the artist. His exhibition was in town.

6. She loves the city. She was born there.

Speaking

9a **Group Work** Play a Game Show. **Group A:** Look at page 137. **Group B:** Look at page 140. Complete the quiz questions.

b **Pair Work** Now work with someone from a different group. Ask your questions. If your partner answers all the questions correctly, he or she wins $1 million.

Reading

1a Complete the news headlines using the words below.

> Saves   Inherits   Takes   Escapes   Deliver   Survives

1. Traffic Police Officer in Bangkok Helps to _____ Baby in Car
2. Lost Driver _____ a Wrong Turn for 5,000 Miles
3. Circus Monkey _____ and Destroys a Restaurant
4. Top Chef _____ Giant Lobster from Cooking Pot
5. Sailor _____ Four Months at Sea
6. Cat _____ $350,000 House and $100,000 from Owner

b **Pair Work** Match the headlines from Exercise 1a to the pictures. Write the number in the box. Then discuss what you think happened in each situation.

A ☐

B ☐

C ☐

D ☐

2a Read the news stories (A–D). Write the correct headline from Exercise 1a for each story.

A
_____

A nervous driver who went on a day trip to Calais ended up in Gibraltar after a five-day mystery tour. Mrs. Bright was planning to go to France to buy some wine. However, as she was driving around Calais looking for the supermarket, she took a wrong turn and lost her way. Without a map and unable to speak French, she was too embarrassed to ask for directions, and eventually she found herself in Gibraltar.

C
_____

Bangkok traffic police sergeant Sakchai Kodayan helped to deliver another baby yesterday. "I was taking a break in a café when a taxi driver shouted for help," said Sakchai. "His passenger was having a baby. It was a boy. The woman said she would name him Sakchai as a way to say thank me." Sakchai has so far assisted with the birth of 28 babies.

B
_____

A giant lobster has been saved from the cooking pot and returned to the sea. Chef Anton Gretzky said he was planning to serve the lobster at his restaurant but decided he couldn't boil such a fine creature. Staff from the Aquarium Restaurant in Victoria, Australia, took the lobster, named Billy, to the coast to free him. Gretzky said: "He has been on this Earth much longer than I have."

D
_____

A monkey, who escaped from a local circus, caused $10,000 of damage to a pizzeria in Lehre, Germany. The monkey, named Lala, was sitting in the restaurant bathroom when the owner found her. Lala dropped a vase, then started throwing paper towels around, and finally turned on the water faucets and flooded the restaurant.

2b Write the letter of the story or stories from Exercise 2a next to the topics below. Then compare your answers with a partner.

_B, D_ 1. restaurants   _____ 3. animals   _____ 5. babies

_____ 2. travel   _____ 4. people getting lost

3 **Pair Work** Read the stories again. Discuss the answers to the questions.

1. a. Where did Mrs. Bright want to go?
   b. Why didn't she ask for directions?
2. a. Where did the monkey come from?
   b. What damage did the monkey do?
3. a. Why didn't the chef cook the lobster?
   b. What did the chef do with the lobster?
4. a. What is Sakchai Kodayan's job?
   b. Why did the woman name her son Sakchai?

4a Match the collocations from the stories (1–4) to the correct definitions (a–d).

Collocation	Definition
_____ 1. took a wrong turn	a. stop working for a short time
_____ 2. caused ($10,000 of) damage to	b. go or give back to
_____ 3. returned to (the sea)	c. drive in the wrong direction
_____ 4. taking a break	d. break something by physically attacking it

b **Pair Work** Without looking at the stories, use the phrases above to retell them in your own words.

c Discuss. Which stories did you find most interesting? Explain your answer. What interesting stories have you heard about recently?

Pronunciation | past tense -ed endings

5a ▶1.11 Listen to the past tense forms of these regular verbs.

/t/	/d/	/ɪd/
escaped	saved	inherited
placed	delivered	decided
washed	survived	waited

b Listen again and repeat.

c Circle the correct answer.
We pronounce the past ending /ɪd/ for:

a. verbs ending in *t* or *d*.   b. verbs ending in *p*.

d ▶1.12 Listen and write the sentences you hear.

1. _____
2. _____
3. _____
4. _____
5. _____
6. _____

Grammar | simple past and past continuous

6a Read the sentences. Do the underlined verbs describe something completed or
something still in progress? _____

 a. Mrs. Bright <u>was planning</u> to go to France . . .   b. She <u>was driving</u> around Calais . . .

b Read the Active Grammar box. Then underline more examples of the past continuous in
the stories in Exercise 2a on page 26.

> ## Active Grammar
>
> 1. Use the past continuous and simple past together to say that something happened in the
>   middle of a longer action.
>   *I **was taking** a break in a café when a taxi driver **shouted** for help.*
>
> 2. The past continuous is often used to set the scene at the beginning of an article or story.
>   *This happened about eight years ago when I **was studying** for my degree. I **was feeling** a
>   bit tired and . . .*
>
> 3. Remember: Some verbs are not normally used in the continuous form.

See Reference page 128

7 Complete the sentences using the cues and the simple past or the past continuous.

 1. I _____ (work) in a school in Seoul when I _____ (meet) my boyfriend.

 2. When I _____ (be) a child, I _____ (like) swimming.

 3. My sister _____ (arrive) just as I _____ (cook) some lunch.

 4. I _____ (know) I wanted to marry him the first time I _____ (meet) him.

 5. He _____ (not break) his arm while he _____ (play) baseball.
    He _____ (fall) down the stairs.

 6. I _____ (check) on the children and both of them _____ (sleep).

8 The picture shows the beginning of a story.
Write the first four sentences of the story.

> It was raining hard. I was
> waiting for the bus to . . .

Writing

9a Choose one of the events in the box and
think about these questions. Write notes.

 1. What were you doing when it happened?

 2. Where were you living/staying when it happened?

 3. What were you thinking about when it happened?

- you received good news
- you received test grades
- something important happened
- an interesting event

b Group Work Tell other students about your event.

10 Write a short paragraph describing your event.

Extra Vocabulary Study and
Extra Listening Activity
in *ACTIVEBOOK*

Review

1 Complete the sentences with the verbs from the box. Decide if you need the active voice or the passive voice.

> give   call   sell   ~~read~~   make   invent   speak

Ex: It's a funny book, and it can __be read__ by children or adults.

1. Wine _____ from grapes.
2. Since 2002 we _____ over $40,000 by the government to improve our services.
3. After the accident, somebody _____ an ambulance, and the girl went to the hospital.
4. Yesterday we _____ this painting to an art gallery for $1 million!
5. Paper _____ by the Chinese over 2,000 years ago.
6. Four languages _____ in Switzerland.

2a Complete the TV schedule with the correct relative pronouns from the box.

> who   where   which   when   whose

7:30	**Brothers in Arms:** Marlon is a lawyer __whose__ (1.) brother has escaped from prison. He faces a dilemma _____ (2.) he realizes Eddie wants to live with him.
8:00	**Home Questions:** The game show _____ (3.) asks contestants questions about the place _____ (4.) they were born.
8:30	**Big Year:** Roy Johns speaks to the people _____ (5.) have made history this year. Guests include Milly Cheiz, a doctor _____ (6.) anti-cancer treatment is being tested in Australia, and Moses Kenui, an athlete _____ (7.) shocked the world _____ (8.) he broke four athletic records in one year.
9:30	**News**
10:00	**Restaurant:** Follows the progress of two restaurants _____ (9.) famous chefs have visited. They both opened last year—one in Watertown, a town _____ (10.) there is 60% unemployment, and one in Hillsdale, a city _____ (11.) the rich are happy to pay $350 for dinner.
11:00	**Fright Kids:** Comedy horror film about a woman _____ (12.) has twins.

b In which two sentences in Exercise 2a can you omit the relative pronoun? _____ In which sentences can you use *that*? _____

3 Complete the sentences. Circle the correct choices.

Ex: We first (met)/were meeting Irina when we traveled/(were traveling) across Russia.

1. I *was/was being* at school when I *started/was starting* learning French.
2. A: What *did you do/were you doing* this time yesterday?
   B: I *watch/was watching* a documentary.
3. A: *Did they win/Were they winning* when you left the game?
   B: No. They *lost/were losing* 2 – 1, but there were still 20 minutes left.
4. A: *Did you see/Were you seeing* our new boss at the conference?
   B: Yes. He *wore/was wearing* a white suit. *Didn't you notice/Were you noticing* him?

Communication | debate the value of news stories

4 **SPEAKING EXCHANGE** You are one of the editors of a Sunday newspaper.

   Group A: Read your role on page 137.

   Group B: Read your role on page 139.

   Group C: Read your role on page 141.

5 In your groups, decide which six stories from the list below should go on the front page of this week's paper. Look at the How To box on page 22 to help you give your opinions for choosing the stories.

> What do you think?   I'm not sure about that.   In my opinion . . .

1. **Skirts for Men Come Into Fashion**

2. **Doctors Discover a Cure for AIDS**

3. Brad Pitt Stars in World's Most Expensive Movie

4. Talking Mouse Created by Scientists

5. Sandra Bullock Raises $500,000 for Charity

6. **Healthy Chocolate Developed by Food Scientists**

7. **Freak Storm Kills 1,000 in Southern Africa**

8. **Computer Virus Likely to Crash all Computers Worldwide**

9. *Ancient City in Asia Discovered by Archaeologists*

10. **Bill Gates Pays Off All Third World Debts**

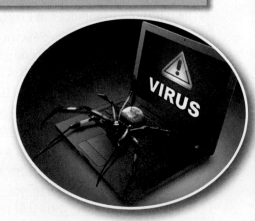

6 **Group Work** As a class, compare your front page choices with those of other groups. Explain your choices.

UNIT 3
Home sweet home

Warm Up

1a Group Work Take turns describing the homes in the photos. Use words from the chart below. Guess which photos are being described.

It is . . .	a house	a duplex	an apartment	a townhouse	
It has . . .	an elevator	stairs	a fireplace	a basement	a garden
	a porch	an attic	a garage	(two) stories	hardwood floors
	a deck	a yard	a balcony	carpeted floors	a pool
It is . . .	spacious	cramped	modern	old-fashioned	sunny	dark

American English	British English
apartment	*flat*
elevator	*lift*

b Pair Work Describe the home that you live in.

Write a letter of complaint
CAN DO ✓

GRAMMAR talking about the future

Reading

1 Describe the photos. How are the houses and rooms different?

2 *Yourhome-Myhome.com* is a website where families can exchange homes with other families for a vacation. Read the property descriptions below and match them to the photos. Write the number of the property in the box.

3a Read the property descriptions again and answer the questions. Write the number of the property on the line.

Which property:

1. is near the old town center? ___1___
2. has outside space? _____
3. has one big bathroom? _____
4. is good for dinner parties? _____
5. has restaurants near the house? _____
6. is near public transportation? _____

b **Pair Work** Which of the two properties would you prefer to live in for a one-month vacation? Why?

Yourhome-Myhome.com

Property 1

A beautiful apartment in Ouro Preto, Brazil. It is on the third floor and is very quiet all day. All you can hear is the sound of the church bells. The apartment is very sunny with large windows. The kitchen is new and opens onto the balcony. The bathroom is spacious. There are two bedrooms, one double and one single, and there is a sofa bed in the living room.

The neighborhood

The apartment is in the old center of the town, two minutes' walk from beautiful 18th and 19th century churches and other historic buildings and a short walk to the business and shopping district. There are plenty of local bars and restaurants serving delicious "cozinha mineira" (a typical dish of the region).

Yourhome-Myhome.com

Property 2

We have a large, charming house with a garden, one hour from the center of Toronto. The house has four bedrooms, each with a bathroom, a large kitchen/eating area, a sitting room, a formal dining room, and a study. The house is old and has a sense of history, and that makes it special.

The neighborhood

There is a daily market and a street full of shops just a ten-minute walk from the house. We are also close to a subway station, which can take you into central Toronto, where you will find all the museums, theaters, shops, and restaurants you could wish for.

Listening

4a ▶ 1.13 Listen to two families talk about their plans for a home exchange. Write *1* (Miller) or *2* (Costa) next to the activities they mention.

_____ 1. visit museums   _____ 4. go shopping

_____ 2. see old churches   _____ 5. visit friends

_____ 3. enjoy the local   _____ 6. enjoy the sun
          food

The Miller family

The Costa family

b Listen again and circle the correct alternatives.

1. **Linda:**   We *'ll/'re going to* see the old churches and historic buildings.

2. **Linda:**   David and I love Brazilian food, so we *will/are going to* try all the local dishes like churrasco and feijoada.

3. **David:**   I really hope this *'ll be/is being* the vacation of a lifetime for us.

4. **Paula:**   . . . we *will spend/'re spending* more than a month in Toronto. We've never been there before.

5. **Interviewer:** I'm sure you *'ll love/'re loving* it.

6. **Paula:**   And I *'m going to/'m doing* do lots of shopping.

7. **Interviewer:** Oh, there are some wonderful shopping areas in Toronto. I *'ll give/am giving* you the address of a great outlet mall.

Grammar | talking about the future

5 Match sentences (1–7) in Exercise 4b to the rules (a–d) in the Active Grammar box.

6 Complete the paragraphs below with words and phrases from the box.

> won't   is going   'm starting   'll
> we'll   're going   's moving

Paula Costa

My mother _____ (1.) in with us next year because she's old and doesn't want to live alone. She _____ (2.) to sell her house, which I hope _____ (3.) be too difficult. She _____ (4.) to share a room with our son for the moment. We aren't too happy about this plan, but I think it _____ (5.) be great because I'll have some help with the baby.

Active Grammar

Use the **present continuous**, ***be going to***, or ***will*** to talk about future plans.

_____ a. Use *be going to* to talk about something you've decided to do. Plans can be general.

_____ b. Use *will* for a decision made at the time of speaking, or an offer.

_____ c. Use the present continuous to talk about arrangements (plans that you have already organized, and for which you have arranged the dates.)

_____ d. Use either *will* or *going to* for predictions.

See Reference page 129

David Miller

I _____ (6.) a new job in June and it's in Ottawa, so I think we _____ (7.) need to move to a new house. We'd like to live somewhere in the suburbs, so we _____ (8.) to look at some of the small towns outside the city. Unfortunately, it's very expensive around there so I'm not sure if _____ (9.) have enough money.

Speaking

7a Write four questions to ask other students about their plans for:

> this evening   their education/career   their home
> this weekend   their (family's) future   their next vacation

b **Pair Work** Ask and answer the questions about your future plans.

    A: *Katia, what are you planning for the weekend?*

    B: *I'm going to visit my aunt. She's having a party to celebrate her . . .*

Listening

8a Look at pictures of the Costa family (A–B) and the Miller family (C–D) during their home exchange. What do you think the problems were?

b ▶1.14 Listen to Paula and David talk about their home exchange. Check your ideas.

c Listen again and write notes. Describe the problems each family had.

	Problems
Costa family	
Miller family	

Writing

9a Read the letter in the Writing Bank on page 145 and do the exercises.

b Write a letter of complaint from David or Paula to *Yourhome-Myhome.com*. Use the pictures in Exercise 8a to help you.

Vocabulary | adjectives describing places

1a Look at the photos of famous cities from around the world. Which cities can you name?

b Find pairs of words in the box that mean the opposite.

tiny	~~unspoiled~~	modern	clean	noisy	peaceful	dull	expensive
ugly	enormous	~~touristy~~	lively	dirty	historical	cheap	picturesque

> *Unspoiled is the opposite of touristy.*

c **Pair Work** Use the adjectives to describe cities or towns you know.

> *Mexico City is enormous.*

Listening

2a ▶1.15 Listen to the conversation. Which city are the people talking about? _____

b Listen again. Complete the sentences by circling the correct word.

1. This is Claudia's *first/second* day in the city.
2. Claudia thinks that the subway is *clean/dirty*.
3. The streets and park were *lively/dull*.
4. Claudia says the buildings are *modern/historical*.
5. The store that she shopped in is *small/large*.
6. The souvenirs she bought were *cheap/expensive*.

Reading

3a **Pair Work** Write a list of what makes a city good or bad to live in. Then compare your list with other students. Which cities do you think are the best in the world?

> Good—beautiful views   Bad—dirty

b Read the article about top cities. Does it mention any of the cities you thought of?

WORLD'S GREATEST CITIES

Vienna, Austria

You've probably heard people boast that their city is the best in the world. Maybe you've even looked around your own city and said the same thing. Have you ever wondered which city is really number one?

William Mercer, one of the world's largest human resources consulting firms, determines that answer every year when they release a list of the world's most livable cities. What makes a city livable? The cities are ranked by many different criteria, for example, the amount of crime, the pleasantness of the weather, and the quality of housing, schools, health care, and recreational opportunities.

So which are the best cities to live in? This year, that honor goes to the city of Vienna in Austria, which ranked number one out of 221 cities. Residents of Vienna enjoy the high degree of safety that the city offers, its strong economy, and its excellent art and cultural institutions, such as its famous opera house. While they are proud of their city, residents point out that Vienna isn't perfect—winters are very gray and smoke from cigarettes can be a problem.

Western European cities dominate the top of the list: Switzerland has three cities in the top ten (Zurich, Geneva, and Bern) and so does Germany (Dusseldorf, Frankfurt, and Munich). Canada also scored well, with Vancouver (#4 tie), Ottawa (#14), Toronto (#16), Montreal (#21), and Calgary (tied with Singapore at #28) ranked the top five cities in North America. Overall, cities in the United States suffered because of high crime rates. The highest ranked US city was Honolulu (#31).

The city of Singapore was the top city in Asia, boosted by its low crime, cleanliness, and the ease of doing business there. Several Japanese cities also ranked high, including Tokyo (#40), Kobe (#41 tie), and Yokohama (#41 tie). In Latin America, three cities cracked the top 100: Montevideo, Uruguay (#76), Buenos Aires, Argentina (#78), and Santiago, Chile (#83).

At the bottom of the list was Baghdad, Iraq (#221), where violence, crime, and breakdowns in public services continue to cause hardship.

World's Most Livable Cities

Score	City	Country
1	Vienna	Austria
2	Zurich	Switzerland
3	Geneva	Switzerland
4 / 5	Vancouver	Canada
	Auckland	New Zealand
6	Dusseldorf	Germany
7 / 8	Munich	Germany
	Frankfurt	Germany
9	Bern	Switzerland
10	Sydney	Australia

4a Read the article again and answer the questions.

1. Who or what is William Mercer? _____
2. How did Mercer compare the cities? _____
3. Which country did best in the survey and why? _____
4. What particular problem do US cities have? _____
5. What positive features resulted in Singapore's high score? _____
6. Which city was last on the list and why? _____

b **Group Work** Discuss. Are you surprised by any of the results? Have you been to any of the cities in the list? What did you think of them?

Grammar | comparatives and superlatives

5 Match the rules (a–i) in the Active Grammar box to these sentences (1–6).

_b_ 1. Zurich is **the nicest** city.

____ 2. Vancouver is a **better** place to live **than** Oslo.

____ 3. Small cities are **easier** to run **than** big ones.

____ 4. London **isn't as organized** as Tokyo.

____ 5. Vienna is **more beautiful than** most cities.

____ 6. Baghdad is **the most dangerous** city.

Active Grammar

	Comparatives	Superlatives
One-syllable adjectives	a. *+ -er than*	b. *+ the -est*
Two (or more)-syllable adjectives	c. *more* + adjective + *than*	d. *the most* + adjective
Two-syllable adjectives ending in *-y*	e. remove *-y* and add *-ier than*	f. *the -iest*
Irregular adjectives (Ex: *bad*)	g. *worse than*	h. *the worst*
For negative comparatives	i. *not as* + adjective + *as*	

See Reference page 129

6 Use the words in parentheses to make comparative or superlative sentences.

Day 24:
Just finished my tour of Russia, which is _____ (1. big) country in the world and one of _____ (2. interesting), too. My flight was much _____ (3. comfortable) this time—big seats! Also, the service was _____ (4. good) last time—free food and drink! When I arrived in Warsaw, the people at Customs were _____ (5. friendly) before (on my first trip I waited an hour while they checked my passport!). Fortunately, Poland isn't _____ (6. cold) as Moscow, which was freezing! This afternoon I had _____ (7. delicious) lunch of my trip so far: a Polish speciality called pieczeń in a great restaurant in _____ (8. old) part of the city.

7 Write sentences about cities you have been to. Compare them using the words from Exercise 1b on page 35 or your own ideas.

Speaking

8a Choose one category of things you are interested in. Write a list of your five favorites for that category.

> Movies: 1. American Beauty 2. Citizen Kane
> 3. Casablanca 4. Avatar 5. The Jungle Book

Categories:
- movies
- music
- food
- actors
- books
- your own idea: _____

b **Group Work** Explain why you chose the things on your list.

> The Jungle Book *is funnier than the other movies on the list—actually I think it's the funniest movie ever. But* Avatar *is much more exciting . . .*

Vocabulary | compound nouns

1 Match a noun from A with a noun from B to make a compound noun. Then write the compound nouns in the chart next to their functions.

A	B
1. washing	a. conditioner
2. air	b. clock
3. DVD	c. machine
4. cell	d. alarm
5. burglar	e. player
6. alarm	f. phone

Compound noun	Function
7. *washing machine*	clean clothes
8.	speak to people
9.	wake up on time
10.	keep the home safe
11.	watch movies
12.	stay cool

Pronunciation | compound nouns: stress

2a ▶1.16 Compound nouns usually have the stress on the first word. If the first word is an *-ing* word, it is *always* stressed. Listen to the words in Exercise 1 and mark the stress.

b Listen again and repeat.

Reading

3 Read the article and circle the best title.

1. New reasons to phone home
2. Cell phones in Europe
3. How phone technology stops crime

Cell phones have completely changed the way we all live. From grandmothers to teenagers, we're talking on the phone and sending text messages more than ever. And with smart phones we're connecting to the Internet—anywhere. But in the future, these phones will do a whole lot more.

Imagine when you leave home for the day. You <u>might</u> accidentally leave the door of the refrigerator open. Don't worry—your cell phone will send you a warning message. What if burglars try to enter your house when you are on vacation? No problem! Your phone will tell you. Imagine it's the middle of summer and you're on your way home. Your phone will allow you to turn on your air conditioner, so that your home will be nice and cool when you arrive.

These ideas <u>will probably</u> be reality very soon. At Japan's Combined Exhibition of Advanced Technologies, companies including Toshiba, Panasonic, and Mitsubishi say they are going to create "intelligent homes" that you can manage with your phone.

Panasonic's Echonet is already available. This piece of technology is the same size as a book. You put it on the kitchen wall and it allows you to communicate with your refrigerator, air conditioner, washing machine, oven, and burglar alarm. It doesn't matter whether you are on a train, on the street, or at the airport. If you have your phone, you can control everything at home.

Mitsubishi plans to develop technology for forgetful shoppers. Let's say you want to know many eggs or tomatoes you have left in your refrigerator. You will be able to use your phone to find out. Your fridge will send your phone a picture and you will be able to figure out what you need.

This technology <u>probably won't</u> be available in the next few years, but it <u>will certainly</u> arrive in our lifetime. And when it does managing your life and home will be a whole lot easier.

4a Read the article again and answer the questions.

1. How did cell phones change our lives? _____
2. When will Echonet be available? _____
3. What will Echonet allow you to do? _____
4. Who is Mitsubishi's new technology for? _____

4b Mark the sentences true (*T*) or false (*F*), according to the article.

_____ 1. You will be able to control your air conditioner with your cell phone.

_____ 2. If you leave your refrigerator door open, your phone will close it.

_____ 3. If burglars come into your house, your phone will call the police.

_____ 4. Echonet is a large piece of technology for the kitchen.

_____ 5. When you are shopping, your phone will communicate with your refrigerator.

Grammar | future possibility

5 Complete the Active Grammar box using the underlined words from the article on page 38.

> ### Active Grammar
>
> **Certain**
>
> ➕ 1. New technology _____ _____/**definitely** change our lives.
>
> ➖ 2. New technology **certainly won't**/**definitely won't** solve all our problems.
>
> **Probable**
>
> ➕ 3. It _____ _____ arrive in Japan first.
>
> ➖ 4. It _____ _____ be cheap.
>
> **Possible**
>
> ➕ 5. Customers **may**/_____/**could** find it difficult to use.
>
> ➖ 6. They **may not**/**might not** understand it.

See Reference page 129

6 Circle the correct choices.

1. She *might/definitely/may to* arrive tomorrow. It depends on her work schedule.

2. *I'll probably/Probably I will/I won't probably* see you later. My class has been canceled.

3. Spain will *win probably/win definitely/probably win* the World Cup again. They have a strong team.

4. David *won't probably/probably won't/will not probably* come to the party. He's sleeping, as usual.

5. They *may come/may to come/come may* to the movie with us if they have time.

7 **Pair Work** Decide if these things will certainly, probably, or possibly happen in the next 20 years. Then complete the sentences.

Ex: Computers __*will definitely*__ get faster.

1. People _____ stop using DVDs. They _____ download all movies from the Internet.

2. Cell phones _____ become smaller.

3. There _____ be robots in every house.

4. People _____ take vacations in space.

5. China's economy _____ become much bigger.

6. Cars and other vehicles _____ run on energy from the sun instead of gasoline.

Listening

8a ▶ 1.17 Listen to three telephone conversations. Complete the chart. Then listen again and check your answers

	Call 1	Call 2	Call 3
Caller's name			
Message			
Caller's phone/fax number			

b **Group Work** Discuss. Have you ever made a phone call in English? Who to? What was it about?

Speaking

9 **SPEAKING EXCHANGE** **Student A:** Look at the role cards below. **Student B:** Look at page 140. Roleplay the telephone conversations. Use expressions from the How To box below.

Student A

ANSWER THE PHONE.

1. You work in an office (Smith and Co.). Your manager is on vacation.
2. You work at Capital Bank. Mr. Jones is in a meeting.
3. You work at hotel reception (Windham Hotel). The hotel guest's line is busy.

CALL YOUR PARTNER.

1. Your partner works in a computer store (E-Tec Computers). Your computer isn't working. Ask for help.
2. Your partner works in an office (Lula Incorporated). Ask to speak to Lula (about an invoice).
3. Your partner works in a school (Ace School of English). Ask to speak to the school director about taking a course.

How To:

Make formal phone calls

Answer the phone	*Hello. Smith and Son. Tracy speaking.*
	Hello. Tracy Brown.
Caller: Say who you want to speak to	*Hello. Is (Yu-Jin) there, please?*
	Hello. I'd like to speak to . . .
Find out who is calling	*(May I ask) who's calling, please?*
	Can I have your name?
Caller: Say who you are and why you are calling	*This is John Fox. I'm calling about . . .*
Try to help	*One moment, please.*
	I'm afraid he's not here at the moment. Would you like to call back later?
	Can I take a message?
Caller: Leave a message	*Could he call me back? My number is . . .*
	Can I leave a message?

Review

1 Circle the correct verb form.

> **Ex:** There is a great show on TV tonight. *Will you* / (Are you going) to watch it?

1. I *am thinking* / *will think* of moving soon.
2. *Will you go* / *Are you going* out tonight?
3. We would love to come and see you this weekend, but Lorenzo *is working* / *will work*.
4. **A:** Who is that at the door? **B:** *I'll go* / *I am going to go* and see.
5. I am too tired to finish my homework now. I think I*'ll do* / *am doing* it in the morning.

2 Rewrite the sentences using the phrases in parentheses so that the meaning stays the same.

> **Ex:** I don't know if I'll finish my essay on time. (might not) __I might not finish my essay on time.__

1. I think I'll stay at home and watch TV. (probably) _____
2. I don't think Mark will be able to come to lunch. (probably won't) _____
3. I am working late tomorrow, so it's possible that I won't see you. (might not) _____
4. I'm almost certain we'll buy an apartment next year. (probably) _____

3 Complete the sentences with a comparative or superlative. Use the words in parentheses.

> **Ex:** The blue car and red car both cost $900. The blue car is __as cheap as__ (as) the red car.

1. He's 6 feet tall and I'm 5 feet 11 inches tall. He's _____ (than) me.
2. No mountain is higher than Everest. Everest is _____ (the) in the world.
3. I found her first book very interesting, but not her second. Her first book was _____ (than) her second.
4. Hospitals were more efficient in the past. Hospitals are not _____ (as) they were in the past.

4 Complete the sentences using a comparative form of the words in the box. Use *than* if necessary.

> ~~quick~~   old-fashioned   picturesque   cold   crowded   quiet

> **Ex:** It takes such a long time to drive to Los Angeles. We usually fly because it's __quicker__ .

1. Bangkok is such a noisy city. I'd prefer to live somewhere _____ .
2. There were so many people on the train. It was _____ usual.
3. Our old apartment was _____ our new one, which is really modern.
4. Look at all the snow! It's much _____ today _____ it was yesterday.
5. Cities are so ugly. I prefer living in the countryside where the views are _____ .

5 Replace each underlined word with a word that has the opposite meaning.

> Dear Juliana,
>   *historical*
> I'm here in El Paso for six months. I'm staying in a house in the ~~modern~~ (1.) part of
> town. The part of town where I'm staying is really clean (2.) and unspoiled (3.),
> and the house is spacious (4.). My room is enormous (5.). During the day it's very
> peaceful (6.). The city center is very lively (7.) at night and I go for a walk
> with friends most evenings. See you next week!
> Clara

Communication | describe your dream house

6 **Pair Work** Look at the photos. What features of each home do you like or not like? Compare the two homes. Which do you like better? Explain your answer.

Dream Home Contest

Would you like us to build your dream home COMPLETELY FREE?!
New Home magazine is giving you the chance.

It's simple to enter. Just tell us about your dream home.

1 Tell as much as you can: What kind of home is it? What features does it have? What words would you use to describe it?

2 Describe the neighborhood or city you want to live in.

7a Read the ad for a contest. What can you win? What do you have to do to enter the contest?

b You are going to enter the contest. Prepare what you will say. Write notes in the chart.

	My dream home
It has . . .	
It is . . .	
The neighborhood/city is . . .	

c **Pair Work** Describe your dream home to your partner.

d **Group Work** Have the contest. Half the class are speakers and half are judges. Then change roles. The speaker with the most votes at the end of the contest wins.

    Speakers: Describe your dream home and neighborhood.

    Judges: Ask questions to get more information. Each judge votes for one speaker as the winner.

UNIT 4
Wealth

Warm Up

1a Read the quotations. Can you match any with a photo?

"Money never made anyone happy."

"Happiness comes from spiritual wealth, not material wealth."

"Time is money."

b Which quotations do you agree or disagree with?

2a Write one thing that:

1. is a waste of money or a good value for the money.

   _____

2. you don't have enough time to do.

   _____

3. you do to use your time wisely.

   _____

4. you spend a lot of money on.

   _____

5. you would do today if you had a lot of money to spare.

   _____

b **Pair Work** Compare your ideas.

Make small talk

GRAMMAR question tags

Reading

1a These words and phrases are in the article. What do you think the article is about?

cheated	trickster	egotistical	good-looking
charm	illegally	pretended	$3 million
prison	mystery	consultant	

b Read the article. Write the headings above the correct paragraph.

Childhood and tricks	Frank today
Wanted all over the world	~~Five happy years~~
The FBI's opinion of Frank	

dicaprio   hanks

catch me if you can

the real Frank Abagnale

The true story of a real fake

a. _Five happy years_

Frank Abagnale, a good-looking young American with more dreams than money, pretended to be first a pilot, then a doctor, and then a lawyer. For five years he traveled the world for free, stayed in expensive hotels, and had relationships with beautiful women. By the age of 21 he had tricked and cheated his way to $2.5 million.

b. _____

In the golden age of James Bond, Abagnale really was an international man of mystery. He was wanted by the FBI and Interpol (International Police) in 26 countries. His good looks and his charm were his most important tools. He dressed well and everybody believed the stories he made up. Leonardo DiCaprio, who played Frank Abagnale in the film *Catch Me if You Can,* said, "Frank Abagnale is one of the greatest actors who has walked the Earth."

c. _____

Abagnale was a lonely child. When his mother, who was French, broke up with his father, a New York shopkeeper, Abagnale had to choose which parent to live with. Instead, at age 16 he dropped out of school, ran away from home, and began his life as an international trickster. He used magnetic ink to change bank code numbers illegally. He managed to steal $40,000 of other customers' money before the banks figured out what he was doing. He also got a Pan Am pilot's uniform by saying that his was lost at the dry cleaner's and that he had an urgent flight. This allowed him to stay in any hotel he wanted; Pan Am always paid the bill. He even pretended to

be a doctor and worked as a hospital administrator for a year. With no formal training, he picked up the skills by reading medical books and watching real doctors at work.

d. _____

Abagnale broke the law repeatedly. He ran out of luck in France, where he spent time in prison, before the FBI finally caught up with him in the US. Despite his crimes, Abagnale never had any enemies. Joseph Shea, the FBI agent who arrested him and later became his friend, said, "I think Frank is close to genius. What he did as a teenager is incredible. His crimes weren't physical. There were no guns, no knives; he just used his brain. He's charming and I admire him. I think he's a good man, but like anybody he wants to better himself, and in this country money is the way to do it. He makes $3 million a year and that's a lot more than I ever made."

e. _____

These days Abagnale doesn't need to trick anybody: he is a successful consultant. He advises companies on security, and he also lectures—for free—at the FBI Academy. It is ironic that he has ended up working for the people who were trying to catch him for so long! He wrote his autobiography in the 1970s and sold the movie rights for $250,000. Abagnale says, "When I was 28 I thought it would be great to have a movie about my life. But when I was 28, like when I was 16, I was egotistical and self-centered. We all grow up." That's true. But not many people grow up like Frank Abagnale.

2 Read the article again and answer the questions.

1. How old was Abagnale when he left home? _____
2. What did he look like? _____
3. How did he get his first $40,000? _____
4. How did he get a pilot's uniform? _____
5. Who was Joseph Shea? _____
6. What does Abagnale do now? _____
7. How does Abagnale feel about his past? _____

Listening

3 ▶ 1.18 Listen to someone retelling Frank Abagnale's story. Find eight mistakes that the speaker makes, according to the article. Compare notes with a partner.

> *The speaker says that Frank Abagnale is English, but he's not. He is American.*

Vocabulary | phrasal verbs

4 Underline phrasal verbs with *up* and *out* in the article and put them in the correct place in the charts.

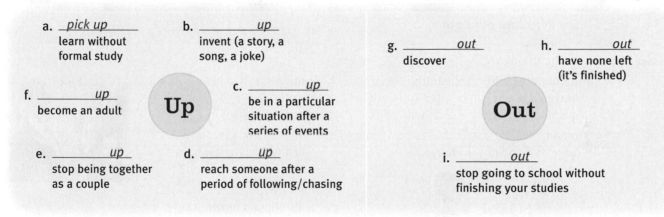

a. _pick up_
learn without formal study

b. _____ _up_
invent (a story, a song, a joke)

f. _____ _up_
become an adult

Up

c. _____ _up_
be in a particular situation after a series of events

e. _____ _up_
stop being together as a couple

d. _____ _up_
reach someone after a period of following/chasing

g. _____ _out_
discover

h. _____ _out_
have none left (it's finished)

Out

i. _____ _out_
stop going to school without finishing your studies

5 Cross out the one sentence ending that is not possible.

		a.	b.	c.
Ex:	He dropped out of . . .	~~tests.~~	school.	college.
1.	I broke up with . . .	my girlfriend.	my relationship.	my husband.
2.	They made up . . .	stories.	an excuse.	acting.
3.	We figured out . . .	what the problem was.	the answer.	wrong.
4.	She picked up . . .	Spanish very quickly.	some information.	a new haircut.
5.	We ran out of . . .	enough milk.	money.	things to do.
6.	I caught up with . . .	my studies.	myself.	you easily.
7.	She ended up . . .	living with me.	work as a doctor.	in Warsaw.

Speaking

6 Discuss.

1. Joseph Shea believes that Frank Abagnale is "a good man." What do *you* think of Abagnale?
2. Abagnale says, "I thought it would be great to have a movie about my life." Would you like a movie about *your* life? Why or why not? Which actor would you choose to play you?

Grammar | question tags

7 Read the Active Grammar box. Then circle the correct choices to complete the rules (1–4).

Active Grammar

To confirm information, question tags are often used.

You are a singer, **aren't** *you?*	*Yes, I* **am.**
You aren't Ecuadorian, **are** *you?*	*No, I'm* **not.**
You work full time, **don't** *you?*	*Yes, I* **do.**
You lived in Lima, **didn't** *you?*	*Yes, I* **did.**
They have arrived, **haven't** *they?*	*Yes, they* **have.**
You can go today, **can't** *you?*	*Yes, I* **can.**
You would like to see her, **wouldn't** *you?*	*Yes, I* **would.**

1. To make question tags, use <u>the main verb</u> / <u>an auxiliary verb</u> .*

2. If there is no auxiliary verb, the question tag uses <u>the main verb</u> / *do, does,* or *did* .*

3. If the question is positive, the question tag is <u>negative</u> / <u>positive</u> .

4. If the question is negative, the question tag is <u>negative</u> / <u>positive</u> .

*The verb *be* acts as an auxiliary verb in question tags.

See Reference page 130

8a Complete the dialogs.

1. **Mr. Charming:** What a beautiful dress! Haven't I seen you before? You work in fashion, _____ you?

   Woman: Yes, I _____. We met at a fashion show in Tokyo.

2. **Man:** Are you familiar with my work?

   Mr. Charming: I've read all your books. You've just written a new one, _____ you?

   Man: Yes, I _____. It's about a movie star.

3. **Mr. Charming:** I love lobster! The food is delicious here, _____ it?

   Woman: Yes, it _____. But I prefer caviar.

b **Pair Work** ▶ 1.19 Listen and check your answers. Then practice the dialogs.

9 Complete the questions with the correct tags.

1. You can speak four languages, _____?
2. You work in a big company, _____?
3. It's warm in here, _____?
4. She has been to Saudi Arabia, _____?
5. We didn't meet last year, _____?
6. You're looking for a new job, _____?
7. You will be here tomorrow, _____?
8. They wouldn't like a drink, _____?

10 **Pair Work** Imagine you are making small talk at a party. Ask and answer the questions in Exercise 9.

Make and respond to invitations CAN DO ✓

GRAMMAR modal verbs of obligation and prohibition

Speaking

1 **Group Work** Discuss.

    1. What do you know about the people in the photos? How did they become rich?

    2. Can you name any other famous wealthy people? What type of reputation do they have? Do people like and admire them?

Sean "Puffy" Combs

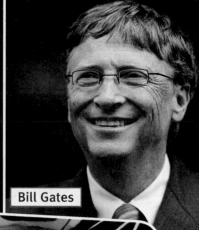
Bill Gates

Estée Lauder

Vocabulary | personal qualities

2a **Pair Work** Check that you understand the expressions in the box.

> be good with numbers   be confident   be ambitious
> be good with people   be extravagant   be cheap
> work long hours   be tolerant   be generous

b Discuss.

    1. For which jobs do you need the qualities in the box?

> *An actor needs to be confident.*

    2. What qualities and habits do you think are necessary to be a successful entrepreneur?

    3. Which qualities do you think you have?

entrepreneur n. someone who starts a company and arranges business deals

Listening

3a ▶1.20 Listen to the first part of a seminar and answer the questions.

    1. Who is the seminar for?

    2. What is the topic?

b ▶1.21 Listen to the rest of the seminar. Circle the expressions in Exercise 2a that the speaker mentions.

c Listen again and complete the notes.

d **Pair Work** Discuss.

    1. Do you agree with the advice given in the seminar? Explain your answer.

    2. Do you think you would be a good entrepreneur? Why or why not?

> Notes
>
> How to be an entrepreneur
>
> 1. Be cheap. You **shouldn't** _____.
>
> 2. You **should** start _____.
>
> 3. You **can't** _____ your money.
>
>   Bill Gates doesn't care about looking good because he **doesn't have to** _____.
>
> 4. Be confident. You **must** _____ in yourself.
>
> 5. You **have to** work _____.

Grammar | modals of obligation and prohibition

4a Put the words in **bold** from the notes in Exercise 3c into the correct column in the Active Grammar box.

> ## Active Grammar
>
> | 1. It is an obligation
(you have no choice).

_____*must*_____ / _____ | 3. It is a good idea
(but you have a choice).

_____ | |
> |---|---|---|
> | 2. It is prohibited
(against the rules).

_____ / _*must not*_ | 4. It isn't a good idea
(but you have a choice).

_____ | 5. It is not necessary. You can do it if
you want to (you have a choice).

*don't (doesn't) have to* |

See Reference page 130

b Read the sentences below. In which sentence do you have a choice? ____ In which sentence is something prohibited? ____

    a. You can't smoke on an airplane.   **b.** You don't have to eat the food on an airplane.

5 Complete the sentences with modals.

    Ex: Vivian has a bad headache. She _*should*_ take a pain reliever.

    1. We _____ wear a suit to work. Dress pants and a shirt with a collar are fine.

    2. You _____ buy your new computer now. There is going to be a big sale next week. You _____ wait until it goes on sale.

    3. You _____ show your company ID card to the security guards at the reception desk. You _____ enter the building without it.

    4. This is a smoke-free hotel. Guests _____ smoke in their rooms. They _____ go outside the building to smoke.

Pronunciation | reduction of sounds

6a ▶1.22 Listen to the sentences. Notice how *to* is pronounced in (*don't*) *have to*. Notice how the *t* is pronounced in *don't/must/can't* in sentences 2, 3, and 4.

    1. You have to buy a ticket.   **3.** I must remember.

    2. You don't have to pay.   **4.** You can't smoke.

b Listen again and repeat.

Speaking

7a **Pair Work** Discuss. What are the qualities of:

    1. a good public speaker?

    2. a good student OR a good teacher?

    3. a good employer OR a good employee?

> *Public speakers should be good with people. They have to be well-prepared.*

b **Group Work** Compare your ideas with another pair.

Writing

8 **Pair Work** Read the letters and emails. Then answer the questions.

1. What is the purpose of each letter and email?
2. What type of work do you think Maria Pesaro and Paul Hunter do?
3. Are the letters and emails formal or informal? How do you know?

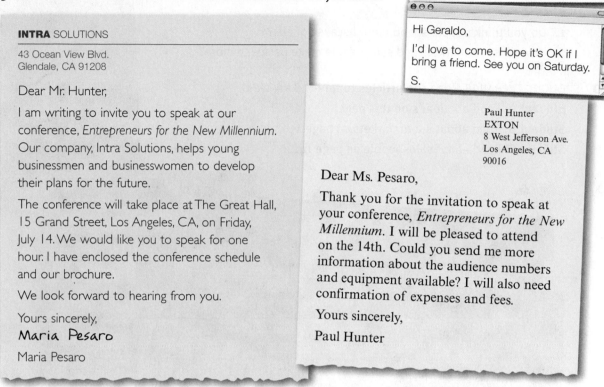

Hi Sophia,

How are you? I'm having a party on Saturday at my place, around 8:00. I've attached a map in case you can't remember how to get there! Hope you can come.   Geraldo

Hi Geraldo,

I'd love to come. Hope it's OK if I bring a friend. See you on Saturday.

S.

INTRA SOLUTIONS

43 Ocean View Blvd.
Glendale, CA 91208

Dear Mr. Hunter,

I am writing to invite you to speak at our conference, *Entrepreneurs for the New Millennium*. Our company, Intra Solutions, helps young businessmen and businesswomen to develop their plans for the future.

The conference will take place at The Great Hall, 15 Grand Street, Los Angeles, CA, on Friday, July 14. We would like you to speak for one hour. I have enclosed the conference schedule and our brochure.

We look forward to hearing from you.

Yours sincerely,

Maria Pesaro

Maria Pesaro

Paul Hunter
EXTON
8 West Jefferson Ave.
Los Angeles, CA
90016

Dear Ms. Pesaro,

Thank you for the invitation to speak at your conference, *Entrepreneurs for the New Millennium*. I will be pleased to attend on the 14th. Could you send me more information about the audience numbers and equipment available? I will also need confirmation of expenses and fees.

Yours sincerely,

Paul Hunter

9a Write a letter inviting a famous person to give a talk at your school. Answer the questions. Use the How To box and Maria's letter in Exercise 8 for ideas.

1. Who will you choose? Why?
2. When will they come?
3. What will they talk about and for how long?

How To:	
Write/respond to an invitation	
Inviting	Informal: *I'm having a party on Saturday, June 21.* *Would you like to come?* Formal: *I am writing to invite you to . . .*
More information	*I have enclosed/attached a map/schedule.* *Can you give me confirmation of . . . ?*
Accepting	Informal: *I'd love to come.* Formal: *I would be happy to attend.*
Refusing	Informal: *Sorry, I can't make it because . . .* Formal: *I am afraid I am unable to attend due to . . .*

b Exchange letters with a partner. Write a letter in response.

Reading

1 Look at the two ads. What products are being advertised? How do the ads make you feel? Do they make you want to buy the products?

2a Discuss.

1. Do you think people spend more because of ads?
2. How do supermarkets and salespeople make us spend more?

b SPEAKING EXCHANGE Read the articles to find the answers.

Student A: Read about ads on this page.
Student B: Read about supermarkets on page 139.
Student C: Read about salespeople on page 141.

How ads persuade you to spend more

Ads focus on either what products do or how the products make us feel. Our emotional response to a product is very important. If the ad makes us feel good—that is, if it has images which we enjoy and remember—then we start to associate good feelings with the product.

We respond well to ads which demonstrate a lifestyle we would like to have. Famous people are often used in ads because of their successful lifestyle. Athletes advertise sports drinks. We buy the drink and hope to enjoy the same success. A survey of 4,000 ads found that ads with celebrities were 10 percent more effective at selling a product than ads without.

Humor is also used, as funny ads are remembered longer. In addition, ad makers appeal to our senses. Unless your mouth waters, a chocolate ad is probably a failure. Advertisers want you to want their product.

Advertising tricks:

- High price: If a product costs a lot of money, it won't necessarily be good quality. It might be just part of its image.
- Reward and punishment: "If you buy this, you will stay young" (the reward) also means "Unless you buy this, you will look old" (the punishment).

3a **SPEAKING EXCHANGE** Now work in groups of three (one Student A, one Student B, and one Student C). Work together to complete the sentences.

> ## Did you know . . . ?
> 1. Supermarkets often _____ to help us relax.
> 2. Supermarkets became very successful after introducing _____ in the 1940s.
> 3. Ads which use _____ are 10% more effective.
> 4. Ads are more memorable if they are _____.
> 5. Good salespeople can sell _____, to _____, at _____.
> 6. Salespeople may try to "mirror" the _____ of a buyer.

b Does any of the information surprise you?

Vocabulary | opposites

4a Write the opposites using the words in the box.

> punishment   sell   success   ~~fail~~   consumer   reward   buyer   produce

Verbs

Ex: succeed/ _fail_

1. _____ /punish
2. buy/ _____
3. _____ /consume (a product)

Nouns

4. _____ /failure
5. reward/ _____
6. _____ /seller
7. producer/ _____

b Complete each sentence with a word from Exercise 4a.

1. Well done. You can have a _____ for passing your tests.
2. Teachers sometimes _____ students by giving them extra work to do.
3. The new advertising campaign was a complete _____. Sales have been terrible.
4. His first book was a great _____. It sold over a million copies.
5. Starting a business isn't easy. It is estimated that 40% of new businesses _____ within three years.

Pronunciation | word stress

5a ▶1.23 Listen to the pairs of words from Exercise 4a and mark the main stress.

Ex: *suc<u>ceed</u>   <u>fail</u>*

b Listen again and repeat.

Speaking

6 **Group Work** Discuss.

1. What are your favorite and least favorite ads? Explain why you think each ad is a success or failure.
2. Do you prefer shopping at supermarkets or at small, specialized shops? Why?
3. Have you ever bought something that you didn't really need because of a good salesperson?
4. Do you think companies should advertise products that are bad for your health?

Grammar | factual conditional with *if/when/unless/as soon as*

7 Read the example sentences (1–6) in the Active Grammar box. Then circle the correct choices to complete the rules (a–e).

Active Grammar

1. **If** *customers think of a salesperson as a friend, they will probably keep coming back.*
2. **If** *I buy a lot now, I won't have to come back later.*
3. *Supermarkets will usually offer Asian pears* **when** *they are in season.*
4. **As soon as** *you walk into the shop, you can smell bread and coffee.*
5. **Unless** *you buy this (face cream), you will look old.*
6. *I will call you* **unless** *it* **is** *too late.* ≠ *I will call you* **if** *it* **is not** *too late.*

Rules

For general present events, *if* and *when* have the same meaning.

    Ex: **If** *an ad is good, you want to buy the product.*

    Ex: **When** *an ad is good, you want to buy the product.*

a. Use *if* + simple present + *will* to talk about <u>real possibilities</u> / <u>imaginary situations</u> in the future.

b. Use <u>if</u> / <u>when</u> for events in the future that are certain.

c. Use <u>if</u> / <u>when</u> for events in the future that are not certain.

d. Use <u>as soon as</u> / <u>unless</u> to emphasize that an event happens immediately.

e. *Unless* + positive verb means the same as <u>if</u> / <u>if not</u> .

See Reference page 130

8 Complete the sentences using the simple present form of the verb and *will* + verb.

1. I _____ (buy) a new car as soon as
   I _____ (can) afford it.

2. When I _____ (see) Tom, I _____
   (tell) him.

3. If you _____ (not pay) the bill on time, you
   _____ (pay) a late fee.

4. I'm sure he _____ (not call) us unless there
   _____ (be) something urgent to discuss.

5. Unless Sandro _____ (find) an apartment
   soon, he _____ (have to) live with his parents.

6. If they _____ (offer) me the job, I _____ (take) it.

Writing

9 Write an ad for an object you want to sell. Give details (price, benefits, etc.).

A/An _____. Only $_____.
If you buy this, _____
_____.

Extra Vocabulary Study and
Extra Listening Activity
in *ACTIVEBOOK*

Review

1 Complete the questions with the correct tag. Then match the questions and answers.

1. I can't park here, _can I_____?
2. I need to call him, _____?
3. The guests will be here soon, _____?
4. She had a headache, _____?
5. This game is boring, _____?
6. I'm a genius, _____?
7. We're going out later, _____?
8. They haven't called yet, _____?

a. No, they haven't.
b. Yes, we are.
c. No, you can't.
d. Yes, it is.
e. No, you're not.
f. Yes, you do.
g. Yes, they will.
h. Yes, she did.

2 Circle the correct choice to complete each sentence.

1. Children under 16 *don't have to/must not* smoke in England. It's illegal.
2. You *don't have to/can't* eat if you don't want to. It's your choice.
3. You *don't have to/must not* be late for work.
4. Ken's so rich he *doesn't have to/can't* work.
5. We *don't have to/must not* miss the last bus.
6. Mariko *doesn't have to/can't* work on Sundays, but she often goes into the office.

3 Complete the sentences with *if, when,* or *unless.*

1. We haven't booked our accommodations. We'll find a hotel _____ we arrive.
2. _____ the weather's nice, it's not worth going to the park.
3. _____ you like action films, you'll love *The Matrix*. The fight scenes are incredible.
4. I'll go home with you _____ you're going to work late again tonight.
5. She'll never pass the test _____ she starts working hard.
6. We'll talk about the new products _____ the conference finishes.
7. You won't feel good _____ you do some exercise every week.
8. I'm leaving early. I'll call you _____ I get home.

4 Complete the sentences with the words in the box.

> ad   spare   picked   value   up   success   numbers

1. I can't even buy you a coffee because I don't have any money to _____.
2. This computer only cost me $400. Do you think that's a good _____?
3. A: What's wrong with Joe?
   B: He's just broken _____ with his girlfriend.
4. A: I didn't know you could speak Russian.
   B: Yes, I _____ it up when I was living there.
5. My wife deals with the money for the business, because I'm not very good with _____.
6. The show was a great _____. More than 600 people came to see it.
7. We need to find a new roommate, so we're putting an _____ in the local paper.

Communication | talk about the best uses of money

A Nicole Kidman's Chanel No. 5 ad

B *Spider-Man 3*

C Van Gogh's *The Sunflowers*

5 Look at the photos. Which activity or thing do you think was the most expensive? Read the Fact sheet to check your answers.

6a `Group Work`

    Group A: Choose three facts from the sheet. Explain why you think these are a terrible waste of money. How do you think this money should be spent?

    Group B: Choose three facts from the sheet. Think of reasons why it was a good idea to spend this money.

b `Pair Work` Work with a student from the other group. Discuss your facts and why you think it was a waste of money or worth spending this money.

7a `Group Work` Are you a money-waster or a money-saver? Write a short questionnaire (five or six questions) to decide if someone is a waster or a saver.

> If someone gives you some money for your birthday, what do you do with it?

b Ask and answer your questions with students from another group.

Fact Sheet

The Millennium Bug: Around the world, over $600 billion was spent on updating computer systems to prepare for the new millennium. Everyone thought that the new date would cause computers to crash. No major problems were reported.

D Neil Armstrong on the moon

Man on the moon: It cost the US approximately $2.2 billion (which is around $40–50 billion in today's money) to send a man to the moon.

Movies: The most expensive movie ever made was *Spider-Man 3*. It cost $258 million.

Painting: *The Sunflowers* by Vincent Van Gogh was sold for $39.9 million at Christie's in London in March 1987.

Cars: The Meitec Corporation of Japan paid $15 million for a 1931 Bugatti Type 41 "Royale" Sports Coupe in 1990.

SETI: Paul Allen, co-founder of Microsoft, donated $11.5 million to SETI (Search for Extraterrestrial Intelligence) for a new, powerful telescope to look for aliens. In the 1980s the US government spent around $2 million a year to fund SETI.

Advertising: Actress Nicole Kidman was paid $3.71 million for a four-minute Chanel No. 5 advertisement in 2004.

Phone number: The phone number 8888 8888 was bought by Sichuan Airlines Co. Ltd (China) for $280,723. Why? The number eight is a lucky number in China.

Forest Lawn Library
Self Checkout
August,29,2017 12:42

39065110581319   9/19/2017
Vocabulary boosters : workbook 1

39065145486005   9/19/2017
English in common 4 : with activebook

Total   **2 item(s)**

You have 0 item(s) ready for pickup

To check your card and renew items

go to www.calgarylibrary.ca

or call 403-262-2928

Warm Up

1   Do you do any of the activities in the photos in your spare time? What activities do you enjoy the most? Explain why you like them.

2   Match the activities and equipment in the box to the correct verbs in the chart.

cards	skiing	fishing	aerobics	bicycling	computer games
yoga	soccer	puzzles	jogging	swimming	martial arts
chess	guitar	exercise	dancing	volleyball	

Play	Go	Do
cards		

Suggest and respond to ideas

GRAMMAR present perfect and present perfect continuous

Pablo Picasso

Steven Spielberg

Sigmund Freud

Lady Gaga

Speaking

1 **Pair Work** Discuss.

   1. What do you know about the people in the photos? In what ways are/were they creative people?
   2. Which creative people do you admire?
   3. Do you do anything creative?

2a Check the activities that you have done in your life.

____ 1. written a poem/song/story

____ 2. made something with your hands

____ 3. painted a picture

____ 4. had an idea to improve conditions at work

____ 5. decorated a room

____ 6. changed the rules of a game to improve it

____ 7. created a new recipe

____ 8. entertained young children for several hours

b **Group Work** Find people in your class who have done the activities in Exercise 2a. Ask follow-up questions to get more information. Tell the class what you discovered about your partners.

> *When did you do it?*   *Where were you?*

Listening

3a ▶1.24 Listen to three people talking about their own creativity. Which activities from Exercise 2a do they mention?

b Listen again. Which speaker says these phrases?

____ 1. I've made lots of beautiful things.

____ 2. I've been playing with my three children . . . that's why the room's a mess.

____ 3. I've made up a lot of my own recipes.

____ 4. We've invented a new game.

____ 5. I've been taking classes . . . for three months.

____ 6. I've been trying to open my own restaurant for the last few years.

Grammar | present perfect and present perfect continuous

4a Read the Active Grammar box. Complete the rules by circling the correct choices.

> ### Active Grammar
>
> Use the **present perfect** for actions which began in the past and continue now.
>
> Use the **present perfect continuous:**
>
> 1. to emphasize that the action is / isn't finished.
>   *I've been trying to start my own business.* (I'm still trying now)
>
> 2. to talk about a recently started / finished activity. We can see the results.
>   *We've been running.* (Result: We're hot and tired)
>
> 3. to emphasize the activity / result, often with *How long . . . ?*
>   *How long **have** you **been reading** this book?* (focus on the activity)
>   *How many chapters **have** you **read**?* (focus on the result)
>
> **present perfect continuous form:** *have* or *has* + *been* + *-ing*

See Reference page 131

b Look at the sentences in Exercise 3b on page 56. Answer the questions.

1. Which sentences use the present perfect and which use the present perfect continuous?
2. Which rules (1, 2, or 3) do they follow?

5 Complete the sentences using the present perfect or present perfect continuous form of the verbs in parentheses.

1. Oh, no! You _____ (break) the window!
2. I _____ (not wash) the dishes yet. I'll do them later.
3. She _____ (write) her novel this afternoon.
4. How long _____ you _____ (wait) for the bus?
5. I _____ (not see) Marta this morning. Maybe she's sick.
6. The kids _____ (eat) chocolate all day. That's why they have stomachaches!
7. How long _____ you _____ (study) Chinese?

Speaking

6a Complete the sentences so they are true for you.

1. I've been working for _____.
2. I've been living in _____ since _____.
3. I've been studying English for _____.
4. I've been playing _____ for _____.

b **Pair Work** Use Exercise 6a to ask and answer questions with your partner.

> *What's your hobby?*   *Chess.*   *Really? How long have you been playing chess?*

Reading

7   Read the article and answer the questions below.

Three ways to become (more) creative

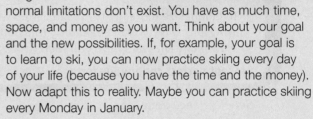

Most people believe they don't have much imagination. They are wrong. Everyone has imagination, but most of us, once we become adults, forget how to access it. Creativity isn't always connected with great works of art or ideas. People at work and in their free time routinely think of creative ways to solve problems. Maybe you have a goal to achieve, a tricky question to answer, or just want to expand your mind! Here are three techniques to help you become more creative.

Making connections

This technique involves taking unrelated ideas and trying to find links between them. First, think about the problem you need to solve. Then think of any random image, word, idea, or object. Next, brainstorm a list of words that you associate with this object, writing as many as you can. Finally, relate the words you listed to the problem. For example, imagine that you need to buy a gift for a friend but can't think of an original idea. Thinking of a random object, you choose the word *candle*. From this word, you brainstorm the words *match*, *light*, *fire*, *wax*, *night*, and *silence*. Relating the word match to the problem gives you the idea to buy

him tickets to a tennis match or treat him to a night out.

No limits!

Imagine that normal limitations don't exist. You have as much time, space, and money as you want. Think about your goal and the new possibilities. If, for example, your goal is to learn to ski, you can now practice skiing every day of your life (because you have the time and the money). Now adapt this to reality. Maybe you can practice skiing every Monday in January.

Be someone else!

Look at a situation from a different point of view. Good negotiators use this technique in business, and so do writers. Fiction writers often imagine they are the characters in their books. They ask questions: What does this character want? What does she dream about? If your goal involves other people, put yourself "in their shoes."

1. Which statement is true?
   a. Most people aren't imaginative.
   b. Only children are imaginative.
   c. We are all imaginative.

2. How does the first technique work?
   a. You link your problem with an image or word.
   b. You link your problem with the word *match*.
   c. You have to think of a present for a friend.

3. In the second technique, what should you imagine?
   a. That you are rich.
   b. That you aren't limited in any way.
   c. That you can ski.

4. What do you do in the third technique?
   a. Imagine you are a negotiator.
   b. Imagine you are a different person.
   c. Imagine you are a fiction writer.

Speaking

8a   **SPEAKING EXCHANGE** Read the problems on page 137. Use one of the creativity techniques in the article to think of possible solutions. Use language in the How To box to suggest and respond to ideas.

b   Tell the class what you discussed, what technique you used, and what solutions you found.

c   As a class, vote on the best solution to each problem.

How To:

Suggest and respond to ideas

Presenting an idea	*Why don't we _____ . . . ?*
	Should we try _____ ing . . . ?
Accepting	*That's a good idea.*
	OK, let's go with that.
Rejecting	*The problem with that is . . .*
	I'm not sure about that.
Presenting an alternative	*Wouldn't it be better to _____ . . . ?*
	Or we could try _____ ing . . . .

Describe a movie or book

GRAMMAR verb patterns with *-ing* or infinitive

A

B

C

Vocabulary | describing movies and books

1 **Group Work** Discuss.

1. Do you recognize the characters in the photos? What movies were they in?

2. Have you seen any of the movies or read the books? What did you think of them?

2 Are these statements about a book, a movie, or both? Which one? What do the words and phrases in bold mean?

Ex: "I liked the **plot**, especially the part about the ring."
book, movie—The Lord of the Rings. Plot = story.

1. "The **soundtrack** was excellent – rock and roll, which is very strange for a Shakespeare play."

2. "The **main character** is Don Vito Corleone, a mafia boss."

3. "It **was written by** JRR Tolkien in 1954."

4. "The **descriptions** of the imaginary place called Middle Earth were beautiful."

5. "It **is set in** Verona in Italy and **is about** two young lovers."

6. "It **was directed by** Francis Ford Coppola."

7. "It **stars** Marlon Brando as the Godfather."

Speaking

3a Choose a movie or book that you are familiar with. On a separate sheet of paper, complete the sentences in the How To box.

b **Group Work** Describe your book or movie to other students. Talk about what you liked or disliked. Explain why you recommend or don't recommend it.

How To:	
Describe a movie or book	
The basics	*It's called . . .* *It's set in . . .* *It's about . . .*
The people	*It stars . . .* *The main characters are . . .* *It was directed/written by . . .*
Talk about particular things you liked/disliked	*The soundtrack was . . .* *The plot is . . .* *The descriptions of (her dreams) are . . .*
Recommend it/ Don't recommend it	*I would really recommend this.* *It's not really worth seeing/reading.*

Pronunciation | vowels /æ/, /ɛ/, and /ɑ/

4a Look at the picture. What do you think is happening?

b Find as many objects in the picture as you can which have the sounds /æ/ as in apple, /ɛ/ as in hen, and /ɑ/ as in car. Write the words in the correct column.

/æ/	/ɛ/	/ɑ/

c **Pair Work** Compare your charts.

5a ▶1.25 Listen and check the sentences you hear.

1. ____ **a.** I saw the man.
   ____ **b.** I saw the men.

2. ____ **a.** She lost her heart.
   ____ **b.** She lost her hat.

3. ____ **a.** I like the rat.
   ____ **b.** I like the red.

4. ____ **a.** He ran after the car.
   ____ **b.** He ran after the cat.

b Listen again and repeat.

Listening

6a Hannah Cheung is a film-maker. In September 2011 she timed everything she did for one month for a movie she is planning to make. Look at the bar graph to see how she spent her free time.

b ▶1.26 Listen to an interview with Hannah. Fill in the four blanks in the bar graph.

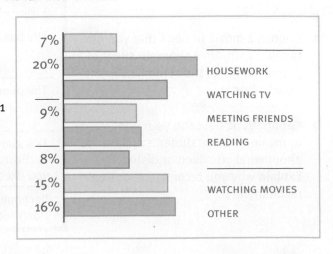

7%	_____
20%	HOUSEWORK
	WATCHING TV
9%	MEETING FRIENDS
	READING
8%	_____
15%	WATCHING MOVIES
16%	OTHER

7 Listen again and complete the notes.

> Hannah says:
> I didn't **expect** to see these results at all.
> I **can't stand** _____ (1.).
> I **don't mind** _____ (2.) housework, but it's not very interesting . . .
> I'd **prefer** _____ (3.) less of that kind of thing.
> I **enjoy** reading, and I always **look forward to** _____ (4.) a new book.
> I **love** cooking, and I **try** _____ (5.) a healthy meal at least four nights a week.
> I often **invite** _____ over _____ (6.) dinner . . .
> I never **manage** _____ (7.) much exercise. I never **seem** to find the time.
> That's one thing I'**d like** _____ (8.).

Grammar | gerunds and infinitives

8 Read the Active Grammar box. Write the words in **bold** from Exercise 7 in the correct column.

Active Grammar

When one verb follows another, the second verb is either a **gerund** (-*ing* form) or an **infinitive** (*to* + verb).

1. Some verbs are followed by a **gerund**. *I can't stand shopping.*
2. Some verbs are followed by an **infinitive**. *I didn't expect to see these results.*
3. Some verbs are followed by an **object + infinitive**. *I told her to call me.*

Verb + gerund	Verb + infinitive	Verb + object + infinitive
can't stand	expect	tell

Some verbs can be followed by a **gerund** or **infinitive**. The meaning sometimes changes.

I remembered to call her. = I called her (I didn't forget) because it was my responsibility.

I remember calling her. = I have a memory of this past action.

See Reference page 131

9 Circle the correct form to complete each sentence. In some cases, both forms are correct.
1. I can't stand _to fish/fishing_. It's so boring!
2. My husband always forgets _to exercise/exercising_. He gained five pounds this month.
3. I love _to practice/practicing_ martial arts. It's a great stress reliever!
4. I dislike _to paint/painting_. I guess I'm just not very creative.
5. I expect _to play/playing_ a lot of golf after I retire.
6. Julio invited me _to go/going_ jogging with him this Saturday.
7. Kyoung-ah loves _to cook/cooking_. She is always trying new recipes.

Speaking

10 **Pair Work** How do you like to spend your spare time? Talk about your likes and dislikes. Use a gerund or infinitive.

Reading

1a Discuss. What are the worst and best meals you have ever had? Do you like food from other countries? What types of food do you like best?

b Read the article about a memorable restaurant. Why do you think the man never found the café again?

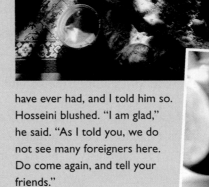

The world's best restaurant

When I was working as an engineer in Iran, I had to visit a factory in Marinjab. It is about 150 miles from Tehran and is a quiet and isolated place. As we drove back along the long road, my colleague and I were both hungry and tired. We didn't have much hope of finding anything to eat, however, as the next town was 80 km ahead. Our only hope was to find a small roadside café, where you are unlikely to get more than some weak tea and a little sugar to eat.

Just then we came to a village made of small huts with flat roofs. Outside one of the huts was a sign "ghahvehkhaneh" (café), so we went in. It was cool inside, and there were men sitting around smoking pipes. The owner came in from the back and greeted us. "Good afternoon," he said, in perfect English. "My name is Hosseini. We do not usually get any foreigners here. It will be a pleasure and an honor to prepare a meal for you."

A lady appeared with a tablecloth and some knives and forks, shortly followed by Hosseini himself, carrying a couple of bowls of soup. Made with spinach and yogurt and served hot, it was the most delicious soup I have ever eaten. Soon, the next course arrived—dolmas, or stuffed vine leaves. These were so delicious I asked Hosseini for the recipe. He replied, "vine leaves and rice." It is not an Iranian dish.

The next course was a Chelo kebab—the national dish of Iran. The meat was marinated in yogurt and spices. We ate in silence and finished with Turkish coffee. There was something almost unreal about the atmosphere of the place. When it was time to go, we asked how much the meal cost, and the price was amazingly cheap. It was a fantastic meal—the best I

have ever had, and I told him so. Hosseini blushed. "I am glad," he said. "As I told you, we do not see many foreigners here. Do come again, and tell your friends."

I told a lot of friends about the meal I had, yet no one believed me. "How could you get such a meal in such a remote place?" a friend asked me.

A few months later, I returned with this friend to exactly the same route. I was determined to show him my special restaurant. We reached the village—I recognized the flat roofs—but there was no sign of the café. It was as if the building had never existed. I asked a villager. "Ghahvehkhaneh?" he said. "There has never been one here in all the time I have been here. And that is 40 years." We drove away disappointed. Naturally, my companion laughed at me. "You have a wonderful imagination," he said. I don't have any explanation. I only know that I definitely had a meal in this village, in a café which, ever since, I have called "the world's best restaurant."

2 Correct seven more factual mistakes in the following summary of the article.

> *an isolated*
> While two engineers, who were hungry, were driving through a busy area in Iran, they stopped in
> a small city. They found a little café. The owner of the café, who spoke a little English, offered to
> serve the men a meal. The meal, which was delicious, was surprisingly expensive. After they had
> finished eating, the restaurant owner asked the engineers to recommend his restaurant to their
> friends. They did this, but the engineer's friends didn't believe it was possible to find such a bad
> restaurant in such a remote area. In the end, the engineer returned to the village with his wife.
> However, when they arrived, they couldn't find the train station. Eventually, they asked a local man
> about the restaurant. He said he had never heard of it, and he had been there for 30 years.

Grammar | count and non-count nouns

3a Read rules 1–2 in the Active Grammar box. Complete the lists of count and non-count nouns
(rule 1) using the words below.

café	sugar	money	rice	coffee	luggage	weather	restaurant
meal	news	water	soup	advice	paper	furniture	information

b Now complete rules 3–5 with *count nouns*, *non-count nouns*, or *both*.

Active Grammar

1. These are common count and non-count nouns.

   Count nouns   **Non-count nouns**
   village   *café*

2. Some non-count nouns are often treated as count nouns because we understand how much
   someone is talking about.

   A: *Can I have **a coffee**, please?*   B: *Sure. Do you take **one sugar** or two?*

   Some of the most common nouns that can be both count and non-count are:
      sugar   water   coffee   tea   chocolate   ice cream

Quantity	None	A small amount	A large amount
3. Use with _____		*a few a couple of*	*many*
4. Use with _____		*not much a little*	*much*
5. Use with _____	*not any*	*some*	*lots of/a lot of*
6. Use *not any* with both count and non-count nouns to express *none*.			

Any, much, and *many* are usually used in negatives and questions.

See Reference page 131

4 **Pair Work** Circle the correct quantifier(s). Then discuss the questions.

1. Do you drink *some/a lot of/a couple of* coffee?
2. How *many/much/little* vegetables can you name?
3. Do you eat *much/a few/a lot* meat?
4. Do you eat *much/little/few* seafood?

Listening

5 ▶ **1.27** Listen to someone describing a restaurant. Check the correct summary.

_____ a. The speaker asks her friend about a new Chinese restaurant.

_____ b. The speaker thinks the Argentinian restaurant is good, but her friend wouldn't like it.

_____ c. The speaker tells her friend about a new vegetarian restaurant which she thinks her friend would like.

_____ d. The speaker is recommending a new Argentinian restaurant to her friend.

6 Listen again and circle any expressions in the How To box that the speaker uses.

Speaking

7a Think about a restaurant you like and would recommend to someone else. Use the How To box to plan what you want to say.

b **Group Work** Tell your group about the restaurant.

Writing

8a Look back at Exercise 2 on page 63 and read the summary again. Underline the linking words used to specify time and sequence, such as _where_, _after_, _finally_, _eventually_.

b Look at the Writing Bank on page 146 and do Exercises 1 and 2.

How To:	
Recommend a restaurant	
Location	_It's on the river/on the main square/ on a small street . . ._
	It's near . . .
Atmosphere	_It's very lively/busy/noisy/romantic._
	It has a bar/live music . . .
Menu	_It specializes in . . ._
	The menu is varied/traditional.
	The (food) is fresh/good quality/ beautifully prepared.
Service	_The service is a little slow._
	The waiters are very friendly/efficient.
Prices	_The prices are reasonable._
	It's quite expensive.
Recommendation	_If you are in (the area), you must go._
	It's worth a visit.
	You'd love it.

Review

1 Circle the correct alternatives.

1. I haven't bought your present yet because I've *worked/been working* all morning.
2. How long have you *known/been knowing* Sally?
3. A: Why are you looking so happy?! B: I've *danced/been dancing*.
4. Hi. I don't think we've *met/been meeting*. I'm Tim.
5. Have you *finished/been finishing* the report already?
6. How many games have you *played/been playing* this season?

2 Complete the dialogs with the correct form of the verbs in parentheses.

1. A: You're late! I _____ (wait) for nearly an hour.

   B: I'm sorry. I _____ (work) late at the office.

2. A: I'm really hungry. I _____ (not eat) all day.

   B: Sit down. I _____ just _____ (finish) making dinner.

3. A: _____ you _____ (speak) to Alexander yet?

   B: No, I haven't. I _____ (try) to call him all week.

4. A: _____ you _____ (leave) any messages for him?

   B: Yes, I _____ (leave) four messages.

5. A: There's paint on your clothes! _____ you _____ (paint)?

   B: Yes, I _____ (remodel) the living room. It's nearly finished.

3 Read the email and write the verbs in parentheses in the correct form.

> Hi Virginia,
>
> I'd like to _check_ (1. check) a few things with you about next week. I am really looking forward to _____ (2. see) you here in NY. The good news is that my roommate, Matt, has agreed _____ (3. give) you his room for the week. He said he would prefer _____ (4. stay) at his girlfriend's place because he can't stand _____ (5. listen) to us talking all night!
>
> The other thing is that on Thursday I have been invited _____ (6. go) to dinner with a new colleague. I am sure you can manage _____ (7. entertain) yourself for one night. There is a lot you can do around here if you don't mind _____ (8. go out) on your own. Remember _____ (9. bring) your cell phone so you can contact me if you get lost. I forgot _____ (10. ask) you what time your train arrives. Let me know and I'll try _____ (11. leave) work early so I can meet you. See you soon!
>
> Love, Felipa

4 Correct the mistakes in the following sentences. There may be more than one mistake, and more than one way to correct it.

   Ex: We went to buy ^*some* a furniture.

1. In the evening I love listening to a music.
2. We went out to lovely restaurant.
3. Hurry up! We don't have many time.
4. I don't think I can come to the concert, because I only have a few money.
5. A: Would you like a milk in your coffee? B: Yes, little.

Communication | talk about something you are good at

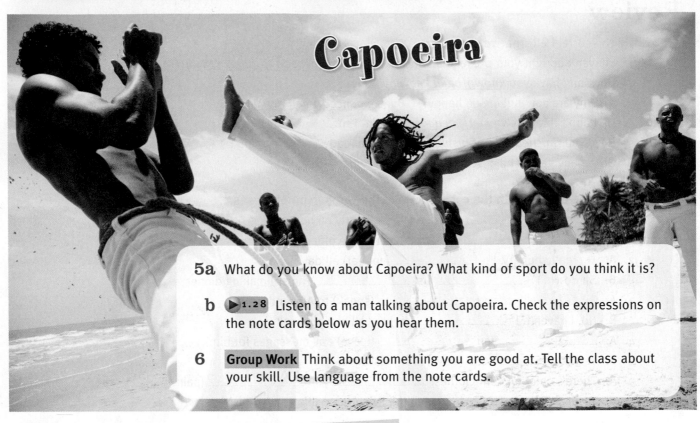

Capoeira

5a What do you know about Capoeira? What kind of sport do you think it is?

b ▶1.28 Listen to a man talking about Capoeira. Check the expressions on the note cards below as you hear them.

6 **Group Work** Think about something you are good at. Tell the class about your skill. Use language from the note cards.

Provide background information

____ Capoeira originated in Brazil.

____ It was started by the African slaves.

____ It's a kind of martial art, but it's also like a dance.

Describe personal qualities necessary

____ You need to be very fit and strong.

____ You should have good control of your body.

____ You often have to use your hands to balance.

Provide other information

____ I have been doing Capoeira for 3 years.

____ I have improved a lot since I first started.

____ I would like to become a trainer and teach other people about this beautiful sport.

Describe main actions/activity

____ Everyone sits around in a circle, singing and playing music, and two people fight in the center.

____ As soon as you see the other person's hand or foot coming toward you, you have to move away quickly.

____ You must be careful the other person doesn't kick you.

____ If the other person kicks you, then you lose.

Describe what happens afterward

____ You can relax and talk about the fight.

____ We often spend the evening together, listening to music.

UNIT 6
Travel tales

Warm Up

1a What types of vacations do the photos show?

adventure	safari	amusement park
sightseeing	cruise	beach
camping	skiing	spa resort

b How would you describe each of these vacations?

romantic	expensive	interesting
convenient	exciting	unforgettable
dangerous	relaxing	peaceful

c **Pair Work** What type of vacation do you prefer? Explain your answer.

> *I prefer beach vacations because they are relaxing.*

Reading

1 Have you been or would you like to go to Africa? Why or why not? What would you expect to see and experience there?

2 Read the excerpt from a travel memoir and answer the questions.

1. Where are Sophie and Daniel? _____

2. Do they experience the things you talked about in Exercise 1? _____

3. How do they like to remember their travels? _____

Travels Across Africa

1 For six hours we shot through the barren landscape of the Karoo desert in South Africa. Just rocks and sand and baking sun. Knowing our journey was ending, Daniel and I just wanted to remember all we had seen 5 and done. He used a camera. I used words. I had already finished three notebooks and was into the fourth, a beautiful leather notebook I'd bought in a market in Mozambique.

Southern Africa was full of stories. And visions. We 10 were almost drunk on sensations. The roaring of the water at Victoria Falls, the impossible silence of the Okavango Delta in Botswana. And then the other things: dogs in the streets, whole families in Soweto living in one room, a kilometer from clean water.

15 As we drove towards the setting sun, a quietness fell over us. The road was empty—we hadn't seen another car for hours. And as I drove, something caught my eye, something moving next to me. I glanced in the mirror

of the car; I glanced sideways to the right, and that was 20 when I saw them. Next to us, by the side of the road, thirty, forty wild horses were racing the car, a cloud of dust rising behind them—brown, muscular horses almost close enough to touch them, to smell their hot breath. I didn't know how long they had been there next to us.

25 I shouted to Dan: "Look!" but he was in a deep sleep, his camera lying useless by his feet. They raced the car for a few seconds, then disappeared far behind us, a memory of heroic forms in the red landscape.

When Daniel woke up an hour later I told him what 30 had happened.

"Wild horses?" he said. "Why didn't you wake me up?"

"I tried. But they were gone after a few seconds."

"Are you sure you didn't dream it?"

"You were the one who was sleeping!"

35 "Typical," he said. "The best photos are the ones we never take."

We checked into a dusty hotel and slept the sleep of the dead.

> " . . . thirty, forty wild horses were racing the car, a cloud of dust rising behind them . . . "

3 Read the excerpt again. Mark the statements true (*T*), false (*F*), or don't know (*?*).

____ 1. They drove slowly through the busy desert.

____ 2. Sophie wrote about her experiences in a notebook.

____ 3. Daniel took photos of Victoria Falls.

____ 4. Daniel was driving when they saw the horses.

____ 5. The horses didn't come near the car.

____ 6. Sophie woke Daniel so that he could take photos of the horses.

Vocabulary | descriptive language

4 **Pair Work** Look at the descriptive language from the excerpt. Circle the correct meanings and answer the questions.

> **Ex: shot through the barren landscape** (line 1)
>
> This means "moved very (fast)/slow."   How do we normally use the word "shoot"?

> *Normally we use the word "shoot" when talking about guns—"He shot someone."*

1. **drunk on sensations** (line 10): This means that you have seen and heard so much that you feel *incredible/bored*. What normally makes people drunk?

2. **roaring of the water** (lines 10–11): This means the water *makes a loud noise/is quiet*. What animal normally roars?

3. **quietness fell over us** (lines 15–16): This means that as they drove *they had a small accident/it became very quiet*. What is something that we usually say "falls"?

4. **caught my eye** (line 17): This means that she *had something in her eye/noticed something and looked at it*. What is something that people normally "catch"?

5. **slept the sleep of the dead** (lines 37–38): This means they slept *very well/badly*. What does "sleep of the dead" suggest?

Grammar | past perfect

5a Read the Active Grammar box and circle the correct choices to complete the rules.

> ## Active Grammar
>
> We **wanted** to remember all we **had seen.**
>   (simple past)   (past perfect)
>
> 1. WhIch action happened first? We <u>saw things</u> / <u>wanted to remember</u>.
>
> 2. Use the <u>past perfect</u> / <u>simple past</u> to show that one event happened before another one in the past.
>
>   We had seen things   we wanted to remember   now
>   ————×————————————×————————————×————→
>
> 3. Make the past perfect using *had* or *hadn't* + <u>past participle</u> / <u>infinitive</u>.

See Reference page 132

b Find examples of the past perfect in the excerpt on page 68.

6 Put the verbs in parentheses into the correct tense.

1. I love bicycling vacations. I _____ (get) my first bike when I was seven.

2. She didn't know the area because she _____ (not live) there since 1983.

3. First I spoke to Sam. Then I _____ (meet) Jo.

4. I was sad when I heard that my old teacher Mr. Cezus _____ (die) two years earlier.

5. We arrived at 8:00 but he _____ (already leave).

6. We were thirsty. We _____ (not drink) anything since 1:00 P.M.

7. Where _____ (you go) after dinner yesterday?

8. I felt sick. Later I realized I _____ (eat) some bad food.

Listening

7a ▶ 2.02 Listen to three people describing the photos. Which photos do they talk about?

A	The Great Wall of China
B	The Grand Canyon
C	Machu Picchu

| D | Egyptian pyramids |
| E | Galapagos Islands |

b **Pair Work** Complete the notes in the chart. Check your answers with a partner.

	Which place?	When did the speaker take the photo?	What had the speaker heard about the place?
Speaker 1			
Speaker 2			
Speaker 3			

c Listen again. Check the phrases you hear in the How To box.

Speaking

8 **SPEAKING EXCHANGE**
Working in pairs, describe a photo you remember well or a photo from page 142. Use the phrases in the How To box. Talk for two minutes.

How To:	
Describe a memorable photo	
Say when and where the photo was taken	____ This photo shows . . . ____ It is/was . . .
Describe what you can see in the photo	____ In the background/foreground, you can see . . . ____ On the left/right there is . . . ____ I think this is . . .
Give background information/Talk about the people in the photo	____ We had been (there) for . . . ____ I was staying . . . ____ We had heard . . . ____ Afterwards, we . . . ____ We felt happy/sad . . . ____ I was very excited . . . ____ We had always wanted to see . . .

Listening

1 ▶2.03 Listen to the dialogs. Where are the travelers?
Circle the correct answer.

1. **a.** at a train station **b.** on a bus **c.** in an airport
2. **a.** in a museum **b.** on a bus **c.** on the street
3. **a.** in a post office **b.** on the street **c.** in a taxi
4. **a.** at an airport **b.** at a bus stop **c.** at a train station
5. **a.** in a restaurant **b.** in a café **c.** in a museum

Pronunciation | intonation: questions

2a ▶2.04 Listen and complete the sentences in the How To box.

How To:	
Get around a new place	
Ask about places in a town	1. *What time does the* _____ ? 2. *Is there a* _____ *near here?* 3. *Can you recommend* _____ ?
Ask for travel information	4. *How much is a* _____ *city center?* 5. *Does this bus go* _____ ?
Be polite	6. *Excuse me. Could you tell me what time* _____ ? 7. *Excuse me. Do you know* _____ ?
Ask for/Give directions	8. *Can you tell me the way to* _____ *, please?* 9. *Just go straight. It's* _____ .

b ▶2.05 Listen to the questions. Why does the intonation start high?

Can you tell me what time the park closes?   *Do you know if there's a post office near here?*

c Listen again and repeat.

Speaking

3 **SPEAKING EXCHANGE** Student A: Look at the role cards below.   **Student B:** Turn to page 139.
Ask and answer questions to find out the information you or your partner needs. Use expressions
from the How To box.

Student A	Student A
Situation 1: You work in a train station ticket office. Tickets to Boston cost: Adult: one way $7.50, round trip $14.00 Child: one way $4.50, round trip $8.50 Trains to Boston leave on the hour and at half past every hour. There are delays today. Trains leave from track 4.	Situation 2: You are in a tourist office. You would like to see the Picasso exhibition at the Tate Modern museum. Find out: 1. how to get to the Tate Modern museum. 2. what time it opens and closes. 3. how much admission costs.

Reading

4a What do you know about Buenos Aires? Mark the statements true (*T*) or false (*F*).

_____ **1.** Buenos Aires is the capital city of Chile.

_____ **2.** Buenos Aires reminds visitors of cities in Europe.

_____ **3.** The city is famous for its excellent seafood restaurants.

_____ **4.** There isn't much happening in Buenos Aires after dark.

_____ **5.** The tango was invented in Buenos Aires.

b Read the travel guide to check your answers.

A _____

B _____

C _____

Buenos Aires
A Quick Guide

Buenos Aires is the capital and largest city of Argentina. Famous for its architecture, cultural activities, and exciting night life, it is one of the most sophisticated cities in Latin America.

So what's it like?

Because of its deep European roots, parts of Buenos Aires look like Barcelona, Paris, and Rome. It has been called "the Paris of South America." But despite its European connections, Buenos Aires has its own unique Latin American character.

What can you do there?

Buenos Aires is a city rich in history, art, culture, and beauty, offering visitors a wide range of activities. The first place to go is Plaza De Mayo, in the heart of the city. All major events in the city's history have occurred in this square, and people continue to gather there today. Several of the city's major landmarks are located around the Plaza, including the Metropolitan Cathedral, the May Pyramid, and the Casa Rosada (Pink House) and Cabildo government buildings.

If you like history, make sure you go to the Recoleta Cemetery, the final resting place of Eva Perón and other famous Argentineans. The cemetery is a city within a city, with over 6,400 tombs constructed in every imaginable style, from Greek temples and Egyptian pyramids to fairy tale–like castles.

Take some time to walk through the city's neighborhoods, called *barrios*, each with its own distinct personality. You'll want to check out the San Telmo *barrio* for its cosmopolitan mixture of Spanish, Italian, and French architecture. It also has excellent cafés, shops, art galleries, and antique markets. And don't leave without visiting some of the great restaurants along the Puerto Madero waterfront. You will enjoy some of the best-tasting beef and red wine in the world.

Finally, you can't miss the night life! Porteños (the nickname for residents of Buenos Aires) are serious dancers. Dance clubs are packed almost every night of the week. You must see the national dance, the tango. Born in the crowded *barrios* of Buenos Aires, it is now practiced everywhere: in clubs, parks, ballrooms—even on the street! Once you feel the rhythm, you'll want to try it yourself. The tango is an elegant and passionate dance, very much like the city of Buenos Aires itself.

D _____

5a Look at the photos. What places, objects, and activities from the travel guide are pictured? Label the photos.

b Pair Work Now cover the travel guide. Can you remember what the guide says about each photo?

c What would you most like to do during a visit to Buenos Aires? Explain why.

Grammar | uses of *like*

6 Write sentences (a–e) to complete the conversations (1–5) in the Active Grammar box.

    a. *What would you like to do?*

    b. *It tastes like chicken.*

    c. *What does it look like?*

    d. *What's it like?*

    e. *What do you like doing on vacation?*

7 Circle three uses of *like* in the travel guide on page 72. Which meanings are used?

    1. _____

    2. _____

    3. _____

8 Complete the dialogs using expressions with *like*.

    1. A: I have never been to Kyoto.
        What _____?

       B: Oh, it is a wonderful city.

    2. A: What _____ do today?

       B: I don't care. You decide.

    3. A: Have you seen the new concert hall?

       B: Yes, it _____ an airport terminal!

    4. A: What _____ most about Bogotá?

       B: I love the La Candelaria neighborhood with all the colorful homes and cafés.

    5. A: I am not sure if I will recognize Mr. Williams. What _____ he _____?

       B: He's tall, with dark hair.

    6. A: Your car _____ fish.

       B: I know. I spilled my lunch in the back seat!

Active Grammar

1. *like* = to enjoy something

    A: _____

    B: *Visiting markets and shopping.*

2. **would like** = want

    A: _____

    B: *I'd like to see the Plaza de Mayo.*

3. **look like** = has the same appearance

    A: _____

    B: *Many people say it reminds them of Paris.*

4. **be like** = describe or give your opinion of this person/thing

    A: _____

    B: *It's a beautiful and energetic city.*

5. (smell/taste/feel) **like** = the same as

    A: *Is that food good?*

    B: *Yes.* _____

See Reference page 132

Writing

9a **Pair Work** Talk about a city you know well. Answer the questions.

    1. What is it like?

    2. What are the people like?

    3. Why do you like or dislike it?

    4. What do you like doing there?

    5. What would you like to change about it?

    6. Does it look like any other cities that you know?

b Write a travel guide to the city you spoke about in Exercise 9a. Recommend things a visitor should do. Use expressions from the guide on page 72 as a model.

c **Group Work** Share your travel guide with other students and read theirs. Which city would you most like to visit? Why?

Reading

1a Look at the pictures below. What kinds of events do you think the article describes?

b Read the article to find out.

Strange things happen when you travel

A whale jumps out of the water and onto your boat. What are the chances of that? A billion to one? There are 139.5 million square miles of ocean and the boat was only 30 feet long. But it happened. A family was sailing off the Australian coast when the whale jumped onto the boat. "Amazing!" we all say. Yes, but unbelievable events happen to travelers every day.

Some of the most incredible travelers, it seems, are pets, who may return home after years away. These stories normally involve cats, though there is a famous story of a dog that traveled 4,800 kilometers from Calcutta, India, to Inverkeithing, Scotland, to return to its master. The dog had been sent to India as a gift to a friend but ran away. To get home, it boarded two different ships and ran over 50 kilometers!

What about the things people lose and find when they are traveling? Rings are at the top of the list. In Hawaii, Ken Da Vico, who is a diver, says he finds about 15 wedding rings a year in the sea. He returns many of them to their owners. Even if a fish eats the ring, there is still hope. There are many cases of rings being found years later inside the stomachs of sharks, mussels, and other kinds of fish. Less common is when the original owner finds the lost ring, as happened when Karen Goode went to the beach and found a ring she had lost ten years before.

But the best beach story involves Roger Lausier, age four, who was saved from drowning on a Salem, Massachusetts beach by a woman named Alice Blaise. Nine years later, on the same beach, a man was drowning. Roger Lausier dived into the water and saved him. It was Alice Blaise's husband.

2 Read the article again and answer the questions.

1. Is the article very serious, semi-serious, or not serious? How do you know?

_____

2. In your opinion, which is the most amazing event in the article?

_____

3. Which events do you think could have a logical explanation?

_____

4. Have you experienced or heard about a strange event?

_____

3 **Pair Work** Retell the stories from the article using the key words to help.
1. family/Australian coast/whale/boat
2. dog/India/Scotland/boat
3. Karen/beach/ring
4. Roger/drowning/saved/Alice/beach/husband

Grammar | articles

4 Read the Active Grammar box. Match the rules (1–6) with these example phrases and sentences (a–f).

- **a.** *Ken Da Vico, who is **a diver**, says . . .*
- **b.** *In **Hawaii**, . . .*
- **c.** *But **the best** beach story involves Roger Lausier . . .*
- **d.** ***Rings** are at the top of the list.*
- **e.** ***A whale** jumps out of the water . . .*
- **f.** ***The dog** had been sent to India.*

Active Grammar

___ 1. Use *a/an* when it's not known which one is being talked about OR it's the first time it has been mentioned.

___ 2. Use *a/an* with jobs.

___ 3. Use *the* when it is known which one is being talked about OR it is the only one.

___ 4. Use *the* with superlatives.

___ 5. Use no article when making generalizations with plural or uncountable nouns.

___ 6. Use no article with most names of people and places.

- Use *the* in names with *States, Kingdom,* and *Republic*: **the** *United States,* **the** *United Kingdom,* **the** *Republic of Korea*
- Use *the* if the name is a plural: **the** *Netherlands,* **the** *Andes,* **the** *Hawaiian Islands*
- Say **the** *south of Spain* and **the** *north of Africa*, but *southern Spain* and *North Africa*
- Use *the* with rivers, seas, oceans, and deserts: *the Pacific Ocean,* **the** *Amazon River*

See Reference page 132

5 Read the stories. Write *a, an, the,* or Ø (nothing) in the spaces.

Lee Jung-Su met his girlfriend, _____ (1.) musician named Jeni, at college in Seoul, and she showed him her favorite guitar. _____ (2.) guitar was _____ (3.) same instrument that Jung-Su's grandfather had played 50 years earlier. It had been lost when _____ (4.) grandfather moved to _____ (5.) new house in Jeju, _____ (6.) island to _____ (7.) south of Korea.

Jeju, Korea

Warsaw, Poland

Michael and Tamara Weisch of New York City went on _____ (8.) two-week vacation to Warsaw. One evening, in _____ (9.) restaurant of _____ (10.) small hotel where they were staying, they started talking to another couple, who, they soon realized, were also named Michael and Tamara Weisch, also from _____ (11.) New York. But _____ (12.) best coincidence of all: both couples had been to _____ (13.) same hotel in Prague exactly a year before.

Listening

6 ▶ 2.06 Listen to the dialogs and complete the sentences.

1. **A:** This diver finds 15 wedding rings a year.

   B: _____ he?

   A: And he returns most of them.

   B: How _____!

2. **A:** A dog went home alone from India to Scotland.

   B: Really? _____?

   A: It traveled by boat and, after months at sea, it ran home.

   B: Huh. That's _____!

3. **A:** I read an amazing story about a family that was sailing.

   B: _____ you? What happened?

   A: A whale jumped onto their boat.

   B: _____? Where?

   A: Near Australia.

4. **A:** Karen Goode found a ring she'd lost ten years ago.

   B: Did _____? How?

   A: It was on the same beach.

   B: _____ incredible!

Pronunciation | intonation: interest and surprise

7a To emphasize words, the vowel sounds may be very long. Which vowels do you think are long in these words or phrases?

1. Really?!   2. That's amazing!   3. Oh no!   4. How awful!

b ▶ 2.07 Listen and check your answers.

c Listen again to the dialogs in Exercise 6 on track 2.06 and notice the intonation.

d **Pair Work** Practice the dialogs. Concentrate on your intonation.

8 How do the listeners in Exercise 6 show they are interested? Read the How To box to check your ideas.

How To:

Show interest and surprise

Use echo questions	*Does he? Did she? Were you?*
Use short expressions	*Really?!/Oh no!*
Use expressions with *That's/How*	*That's amazing!/That's a shame!/How interesting!/How awful!*
Ask a follow-up question	*When? Where? How? Why? What was it like?*

Speaking

9 **SPEAKING EXCHANGE** Student A: Turn to page 140. Student B: Turn to page 141. Read your sentences to each other. Use the How To box to express surprise and interest.

> I love Shakespeare.   Do you?

> Yes. I've seen all 37 of his plays.   Really? Which is your favorite?

Review

1 Circle the correct form.

> **Ex:** When I got to the restaurant, I realized that I *left*/*had left* her phone number at home.

1. By the time she was 18, she *lived*/*had lived* in six countries.
2. On my birthday, when I *got*/*had got* home I found that my husband *had cooked*/*cooked* dinner.
3. That morning, she got up, had breakfast, and *went*/*had gone* to work, as usual.
4. Costa Rica was incredible. I *never saw*/*had never seen* such a beautiful country before.
5. He called twice but no one answered. They *all went*/*had all gone* to bed.
6. When I arrived in Ecuador, my cousins *kissed*/*had kissed* me on the cheek.

2 Put the words in order.

> **Ex:** to/you/Would/something/eat/like/? _Would you like something to eat?_

1. is/What/like/it/? been/there/haven't/I/before/. _____
2. like/I/at/prefer/but/movies/I/watching/the/going/to/theater/home/. _____
   _____
3. looks/sister/you/like/think/Don't/her/Maria/? _____
4. to/what/see/wait/finished/the/house/will/look/when/like/I/it/is/can't/. _____
   _____
5. early/Tim/up/getting/doesn't/like/. _____
6. like/your/is/job/new/What/? _____

3 Do the place names use *the* or not? Complete the chart with the places in the box.

> | | | | | |
> |---|---|---|---|---|
> | ~~Black Sea~~ | Canary Islands | Andes mountains | Czech Republic | Caribbean Sea |
> | Africa | Amazon River | United Arab Emirates | Central America | |
> | Canada | Atlantic Ocean | Mount Kilimanjaro | Sahara Desert | |

Use *the*	Don't use *the*
the Black Sea	

4 Circle the correct choice.

> **Ex:** A: Why do you like this hotel so much?
>
> > B: It's *a hotel*/*the hotel* where I met Dave.

1. A: How was the restaurant?
   B: *The food*/*Food* was wonderful. But it was a little expensive.
2. A: Why don't you go to Japan for your vacation?
   B: I don't like *the airplanes*/*airplanes*.
3. A: Who was Alexander Fleming?
   B: He's *a*/*the* man who discovered penicillin.
4. A: Why didn't you buy a dog?
   B: *The cats*/*Cats* are easier to take care of.
5. A: What happened yesterday?
   B: *The*/*A* strange man knocked on our door and asked for water.

Communication | plan a trip using a travel guide

5 Look at the Bangkok travel guide and find a description of:

1. houses built on the water.
2. a museum that requires at least a half-day visit.
3. a theater where a mask dance is performed.
4. a market where vendors sell from boats.
5. a market that is only open at night.
6. a place that doesn't allow shorts or flip-flops.

6a **Group Work** You are going to plan a day trip for your group in Bangkok. Plan your day, using the travel guide. Plan activities for the morning, afternoon, and evening.

b Tell the class about your plans. Explain why you want to do each activity.

royal barge

Aksra Theater

Khon mask dance

Floating Market

WHAT TO DO IN BANGKOK

Ⓢ SIGHTSEEING

River Cruise. View the many historical sites on the Chao Phraya River by boat, including the **Royal Summer Palace** and the **Wat Yai Chaimongkon temple**. Along the way, see the traditional houses that rise out of the river on wooden stilts. US $35

The Grand Palace and Wat Pra Kaew temple. Visit the center of religious and ceremonial life in Thailand. This palace complex was built in 1782 and contains the most important Buddhist temple in Thailand, famous for its Emerald Buddha—a spectacular dark green statue carved from a single jade stone. No shorts or flip-flops allowed. US $8

Ⓜ MUSEUMS

The National Museum. Dedicate at least half a day to explore this museum. The collections represent all periods of Thai history and give an extraordinary introduction to the country's art and architecture. US $1.50

The Royal Barges National Museum. This outdoor museum displays large barges used by the King of Thailand. Carved out of whole trees and painted with real gold, these boats are only used for very special royal ceremonies. US $4

😊 THEATERS

Aksra Theater. Enter a magical world at this traditional puppet theater. One of Bangkok's must-see attractions, the puppet shows act out Thai folk stories, using traditional dance, martial arts, costumes, and music. 7:00 P.M. daily. US $20

National Theater. See traditional dance and classical Thai drama, as well as music performances. Particularly exciting is the Khon, a Thai mask dance drama. US $13

🛍 SHOPPING

Sukhumvit Road. Bangkok's most famous shopping street has something for everyone—from malls and department stores selling the latest fashions to small shops and sidewalk vendors selling cheap T-shirts and DVDs.

Markets. At the **Damnoen Saduak Floating Market**, produce vendors still sell their goods from traditional flat boats. Adventurous shoppers can find great bargains at the **Pat Pon Night Market** and **Chatuchak Weekend Market**.

UNIT 7
Lifelong learning

Warm Up

1   Which of the learning situations in the photos have you experienced? Which do you think are the most effective?

2   Complete the chart. Make as many verb + noun collocations as possible.

> ~~an assignment~~   a class   a degree   a test   an exercise   homework
> a report card   lessons   notes   research   a tutor   a failing/passing grade

do	take	get
do an assignment		

Describe a learning experience

GRAMMAR subject and object questions

Listening

1a **Pair Work** What do you think the people are doing in the pictures (A–D)?

b ▶2.08 Listen and write the number of the speaker next to the picture. Were your guesses in Exercise 1a incorrect?

2a Which picture (A–D) do these phrases and sentences from the listening refer to?

_____ 1. . . . nobody had time to teach her.

_____ 2. . . . my teacher told me to hold an orange in each hand as I played.

_____ 3. It was really useful.

_____ 4. She wrote lists of verbs and tenses . . .

_____ 5. . . . it was very difficult.

_____ 6. . . . you had to keep the pencil on the paper all the time, so the picture was just one line.

_____ 7. "I'm practicing," she said. "When I can do it standing still, then I'll be ready to start moving forward."

_____ 8. He told us to sit opposite a partner, and draw the person's face without looking.

b Listen again to check your answers.

Vocabulary | education

3a Complete the phrases and expressions with the words and phrases from the box.

steep	strict	heart	up
perfect	by doing	fast	

People

1. a _____ learner
2. a _____ teacher

Ways of learning

3. Practice makes _____.
4. It's a _____ learning curve.
5. learn by _____

6. learn _____
7. pick (something) _____

b **Pair Work** Discuss.

1. Which pictures in Exercise 1a could the phrases and expressions relate to?
2. Do you think the ways of learning described in Exercise 1b are good ideas? Why or why not?

A

B

C

D

4a Think about a good (or bad) learning experience you have had. Make questions from the cues below.

1. What/learn? Why? _____
2. Why/experience/good/bad? _____
3. How/you/learn? _____
4. Easy/difficult to learn? _____
5. How/you/make progress? _____

b Answer the questions. Write notes on a separate sheet of paper.

c **Pair Work** Talk about your experience. Use the How To box and give as much detail as possible.

Reading

5 What do you think is the connection between light bulbs, potato chips, bread, and Post-it™ notes? Read the article to find out.

Mistakes
that work...

People who don't make mistakes are unlikely to learn anything. The best way to learn something is to make mistakes first. Thomas Edison, who invented the light bulb, told his colleagues, "Of the 200 light bulbs that didn't work, every failure told me something I was able to incorporate into the next attempt." Benjamin Franklin, the US statesman and scientist, once said, "I haven't failed; I have had 10,000 ideas that didn't work."

Both these people understood that failures and false starts are conditions of success. In fact, a surprising number of everyday objects had their beginnings in a mistake or a misunderstanding. In 1970, a scientist trying to make a very strong glue created just the opposite. His new glue would stick to objects but could easily be lifted off. The Post-it™ note was born. In 2600 B.C., a tired Egyptian slave invented bread when the dough rose during his sleep. And potato chips were first cooked by a chef in the US when a customer complained that his fried potatoes were not thin enough.

Successful businesspeople have often made big, expensive mistakes in their past. When an employee of IBM made a mistake that cost the company $600,000, Thomas Watson, the chairman, was asked if he would fire the man. "Of course not," he replied. "I have just spent $600,000 training him. I am not going to let another company benefit from his experience."

The important thing to remember is that you need to learn from your mistakes. If you don't, then there is no sense in making them.

6 **Pair Work** Discuss.

1. How were Post-it™ notes, potato chips, and bread "happy accidents"?
2. Why wasn't the IBM employee fired after making a $600,000 mistake?
3. According to the article, what's the best way to learn something? Do you agree with this opinion? Why or why not?
4. Give an example of a time when you learned or didn't learn from a mistake.

Grammar | subject and object questions

7 Look at the Active Grammar box. Circle the correct choices to complete the rules.

Active Grammar

Object questions	Subject questions
What did Thomas Edison invent? Thomas Edison invented the **light bulb**.	**Who** invented the light bulb? **Thomas Edison** invented the light bulb.
1. The light bulb is the <u>subject</u> / <u>object</u> of the question.	3. Thomas Edison is the <u>subject</u> / <u>object</u> of the question.
2. When the *Wh-* question word refers to the object of the question, use:	4. When a *Wh-* word refers to the subject in a question, do not use the auxiliary verb. The word order is the same as the affirmative.
Form: Question word + auxiliary + subject + verb	
What did Benjamin Franklin **say**?	Form: Subject + verb + object **Who wrote** *The Lord of the Rings*?

See Reference page 133

8a **Pair Work** Student A: Look at Quiz A. Student B: Look at Quiz B. On a separate sheet of paper, use the cues to write questions for the statements.

b **SPEAKING EXCHANGE** Student A: Look at the answers to Quiz A on page 139. **Student B:** Look at the answers to Quiz B on page 141. Ask each other your quiz questions. Give 1 point for each correct answer.

Mozart

the Beatles

Quiz A

1. A famous artist painted *Guernica* in 1937. (Who?)

2. Mozart started composing music. (When?)

3. A scientist discovered penicillin in 1928. (Who?)

4. One of the world's greatest scientists lived from 1879–1955. (Which?)

5. A famous city is nicknamed The Big Apple. (Which?)

6. Guglielmo Marconi is credited with an invention. (What invention?)

Quiz B

1. Christopher Columbus discovered these islands in 1492, before he discovered America. (Which?)

2. An Italian artist painted the Sistine Chapel. (Who?)

3. This country has the smallest area of all European countries. (Which?)

4. A famous Beatle wrote the song *Imagine* in 1971. (Who?)

5. John Logie Baird invented something. (What?)

6. This is the world's longest river. (Which?)

Vocabulary | describing teachers

1 What can you remember about your first day at school? How did you feel? What did you think of the teachers?

2a Look at the photos. What do you think these teachers are like?

b **Pair Work** Check your understanding of the words and phrases in the box. Which are the qualities of a good teacher?

Things a teacher does	Things a teacher is
loses his or her temper	patient
talks slowly	boring
asks difficult questions	knowledgeable
punishes students who	understanding
behave badly	inspiring
gives clear answers to	frightening
questions	open-minded

3 Circle the correct choice.

1. Her classes were so *open-minded/boring/inspiring* that everyone fell asleep.

2. Our teacher is very calm. She never *talks slowly/behaves badly/loses her temper*.

3. My teacher is very *patient/knowledgeable/frightening*. He explains things many times.

4. The students know everything about the topic. They are extremely *patient/knowledgeable/open-minded*.

5. When students have problems, Mr. Cruz helps them. He is very *boring/understanding/open-minded*.

6. My French teacher was really *inspiring/boring/frightening*. All of us wanted to speak fluently.

Listening

4a ▶2.09 Listen to two people discussing their teachers. Complete the chart.

	Subject	Good and bad qualities	Other information
Mr. Halsworth			
Mrs. Matthews			
Madame Bouchier			
Mr. Ford			

b Listen again to check your answers.

Grammar | *used to* and *would*

5 Complete the Active Grammar box with the example sentences below.

1. *We would throw paper at him.*
2. *She used to play us Mozart.*
3. *I didn't use to like her lessons at all.*
4. *We'd learn about the stars.*

Active Grammar

1. Use *used to* + verb and *would* + verb to talk about repeated actions in the past which don't happen now.

   a. _____ (action)

   b. _____ (action)

2. Only use *used to/didn't use to* + verb to talk about states in the past.

   c. _____ (state)

   NOT: ~~I wouldn't like her lessons at all.~~

3. *Would* is usually contracted to *'d* in spoken English.

   d. _____

See Reference page 133

6 Read the essay and circle the correct form.

Going to school

I didn't _used to / use to / did_ (1.) like the journey to school.
I _wouldn't / would to / would_ (2.) go by bus, but I was afraid
of the other children. They were bigger than me, and they
used to / wouldn't to / would to (3.) shout at me. I always sat in the
back of the bus, even though it _would be / used to be / used be_ (4.)
the hottest place, and I _wouldn't / didn't use to / would_ (5.) hope
that no one could see me. It's funny to think that those kids were
probably only eight years old, but I _would be / used to be / used be_ (6.)
so frightened.

7 Complete the sentences using *use(d) to* and a verb from the box.

> live   not watch   be   like   not behave   do   not go   eat

1. Did your life _____ very different when you were a child? How?
2. I _____ playing outside with my friends.
3. I _____ TV in the evenings.
4. We _____ in the countryside, but now I live in Vienna.
5. My family _____ to the beach on weekends.
6. Did you _____ ice cream every day?
7. My best friend at school was named Sam. We always _____ our homework together.
8. I _____ very well at school.

Pronunciation | *used to/didn't use to*

8a ▶ 2.10 Listen to the sentences. How are *used to* and *didn't use to* pronounced? Which letters are silent?

1. He used to lose his temper.
2. Did you use to work hard?
3. He used to teach us English.
4. I didn't use to like her class.
5. We didn't use to do our homework.
6. She used to play music for us.

b Listen again and repeat the sentences.

Speaking

9a Think about a good (or bad) teacher from your past. Answer the questions.

1. What did he or she look like? _____
2. What subject did he or she use to teach? _____
3. What did he or she use to do that was so special or bad? _____
4. Did all the students like or dislike this teacher? Why? _____
5. How did this teacher treat you personally? _____
6. Would you like to meet him or her again? Why or why not? _____

b Pair Work Tell your partner about your teacher.

Writing

10 Look at the Writing Bank on page 147 and complete the exercises.

11 Look at this website. On a separate sheet of paper, write about a memorable teacher you have had.

GREAT**TEACHERS**

| Log-in | News | Events |

We are compiling stories of great teachers and the qualities that made them memorable. You can help by submitting a memory of your special teacher. Include:

- Your favorite teacher's name
- The school subject this teacher taught
- The first characteristic that you think of when you remember this teacher
- A specific memory of this teacher
- A description of how this teacher treated you as a student
- An explanation of what made this teacher special

Talk about abilities

GRAMMAR modals of ability, past and present

Vocabulary | aging

1 Match the definitions (a–e) to the words in **bold** in the sentences (1–5).

a. beliefs about how to live one's life (n)

b. old (used to describe people) (adj)

c. to stop working, usually because of old age (v)

d. people who are over the age of 60 (n)

e. a place where people who are too old or too sick to take care of themselves can live (n)

____ 1. My mother's **nursing home** is more like a home than a hospital—she has her own room and shares a living room and kitchen.

____ 2. John will **retire** from his job next month after working for the same company for 35 years.

____ 3. Some employers avoid hiring **senior citizens** because they think they may have trouble using new technology.

____ 4. The fastest-growing group among the **elderly** population is the "oldest old"—age 80 and older.

____ 5. My **personal philosophy** is to never stop learning. It's never too late to learn something new.

Reading

2 **SPEAKING EXCHANGE** Student A: Read about the two people below. Student B: Read about the two people on page 143. As you read, write notes about the topics in the box. Then tell your partner about the people.

> Name   Age   Activity/Achievement   Personal philosophy about being old

It's never too late . . .

Jacob Adler, 93, USA

Jacob discovered the Internet at the ripe age of 87, when his granddaughter gave him an old laptop to use. At first, Jacob struggled to learn how to use the computer. "I wasn't even able to use the mouse. It took me three months before I managed to right-click!" Six years later, he's a master: "Now I can read news from all around the world. I especially like reading newspapers and magazines from Germany, where I grew up."

He also keeps in touch with his eight grandchildren through emails and follows their posts on Facebook. "You know, I was the oldest Facebook user for a while. But now it's some woman in Ireland. She's 102." Recently, Jacob moved to a nursing home. His computer helps him stay connected to his family, some of whom live across the country. "If I weren't online, I couldn't stay in such close contact." Jacob also believes that using the computer keeps his mind sharp. "That's important when you get older. If you let your mind get lazy, forget it, you're done."

Liu Mei-Ling, 72, Taiwan

Mei-Ling always had a passion for cooking. As a mom, she spent many happy hours in the kitchen, cooking delicious meals for her five children, husband, and father-in-law. After she retired from an office job at age 65, Mei-Ling managed to fulfill her life-long dream—she opened her own restaurant. Mei-Ling called her restaurant Jia Ting, which means *family*. It was an immediate success. Customers couldn't get enough of her home-style dishes.

Seven years later, at age 72, she's still full of energy—cooking, planning menus, and researching new recipes. "Sure, I get tired," says Mei-Ling. "When I was younger, I was able to stay on my feet much longer. But I think if you truly believe you can do something, you can succeed. Anyway, it's working for me!" Recently, her granddaughter started helping out in the kitchen. "That gives me such a feeling of purpose and tradition," says Mei-Ling. "I'll be running this restaurant as long as I can."

3 Complete the sentences below with the phrases from the box.

> could cook   couldn't use   managed to learn   wasn't able to run   managed to write
> could swim   couldn't write   was able to start   was able to swim

1. Jacob Adler _____ how to use a computer to stay connected to his family. At first, he _____ a mouse!
2. Liu Mei-Ling _____ very well. After she retired, she _____ her own restaurant.
3. Juan Lopez _____ a book when he was 92 years old. He _____ his book when he was younger.
4. After Jackie Taylor injured her knee, she _____ anymore. However, she _____ .

Grammar | modals of ability, past and present

4 Complete the Active Grammar box with the words and phrases from the box.

> could   were able to   couldn't   can't   weren't able to   didn't manage to

---

Active Grammar

1. To describe general ability in the present, say:

   ⊕ I **can** swim.

   ⊖ She _____ play the violin.

2. To describe general ability in the past, say:

   ⊕ When we were young, we _____ climb trees.
   When I was young, I **was able to** dance for hours.

   ⊖ When I was a teenager, I **couldn't** drive.
   When we were students, we _____ speak French.

3. To describe something that happened at a particular moment in the past, say:

   ⊕ Yesterday, they _____ finish their work early.
   I **managed to** buy the tickets at the last minute.

   ⊖ She **wasn't able to** attend the meeting last week.
   They _____ find a hotel.
   He _____ visit his friends on Sunday.

See Reference page 133

5 Rewrite the sentences using the words in parentheses. Write 2–4 words.

1. In 1994 John Parr finally climbed Mount Everest after eight attempts. (managed)
   John Parr finally _____ Mount Everest in 1994.
2. When he was a child, Orgosky was already a composer. (able)
   Orgosky _____ write music when he was a child.
3. We didn't go. The weather was bad. (weren't) We _____ because of the bad weather.
4. He wasn't able to meet his friends. (couldn't) He _____ his friends.

Pronunciation | negative modals

6 ▶ 2.11 Listen and check the sentences you hear.

_____ 1. a. I could do it.　　　_____ 3. a. I could run fast.　　　_____ 5. a. We could see it.

_____　b. I couldn't do it.　　　_____　b. I couldn't run fast.　　　_____　b. We couldn't see it.

_____ 2. a. He was able to stop.　_____ 4. a. They were able to play.　_____ 6. a. Were you able to go?

_____　b. He wasn't able to stop.　_____　b. They weren't able to play.　_____　b. Weren't you able to go?

Speaking

7 **Pair Work** Ask about your partner's abilities. Check the columns in the table and note any extra information.

> *Can you run five miles?*　　*I can't now, but I could a few years ago.*

 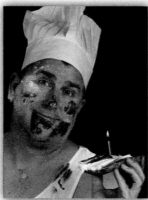 

	Can do now	Could in the past but can't now	Was able to once	Extra information (when, what, where, etc.)
Run five miles				
Make a cake				
Swim for one hour				
Play a musical instrument				
Ride a horse				
Stay up all night				
Sing three songs				
Touch your toes (not bending your knees!)				
Throw with your "wrong" hand				

Review

1   Write questions using the words in parentheses.

Ex: Something went wrong. (what?)   <u>*What went wrong?*</u>

1. Somebody called me last night. (who?) _____

2. He catches the train at 2:00. (when?) _____

3. She ran into one of the offices. (which?) _____

4. He failed the test. (why?) _____

5. Something fell on the floor. (what?) _____

6. They met at a party. (how?) _____

2   Complete the essay with *used to* and a verb from the box.

~~wake up~~	dream	stay	study	have	spend
go out	read	love	stay	get	

When we were children, my sister and I <u>*used to wake up*</u> (1.) at 5:30 in the morning and want to get up. My mother _____ (2.) very angry if we went into her bedroom before it was light. So we _____ (3.) in bed and sing songs until she came to get us. We didn't _____ (4.) much for breakfast, just a piece of toast and glass of milk. I _____ (5.) going to school and playing with all my friends. We didn't _____ (6.) very much, so our grades were never very good. On weekends, I _____ (7.) a lot of time at home. We didn't _____ (8.) much, instead we _____ (9.) at home and help my mother. My father _____ (10.) the newspaper and watch sports on TV. I _____ (11.) of being a famous athlete.

3   Correct the mistakes in five of the sentences.

Ex: Alice used ⌄read books to her sister.
<small>to</small>

1. Sam use to smoke but now he has quit.

2. He didn't use to go to the gym, but now he has started going every week.

3. Tomas would to go to the market every day with his father.

4. Emil used love riding horses on the beach.

5. They'd leave the keys in the door so I could open it.

6. Tom didn't use have a girlfriend, but now he has three!

7. She would play the guitar for me one time when I came to visit.

4   Circle the correct choice.

Ex: We *could/managed not to/(weren't able to)* meet. I was too busy.

1. When he was ten, he *could/manage to/was able* answer difficult math questions.

2. I lost my passport but luckily I *managed to/could/can* find it before my vacation.

3. He *was able to/wasn't able to/didn't manage* get the job because he wasn't qualified.

4. I *can't/could/manage to* ski well before I broke my leg last year.

5. It wasn't easy to pass my driving test, but eventually I *could/managed to/am able to*.

6. Unfortunately, we *could/aren't able to/managed to* give refunds for broken items.

7. He *didn't manage to/could/couldn't* draw when he was young, but now he's an artist.

Communication | tell stories from your childhood

5a ▶2.12 Listen to a childhood story. Which photo illustrates the story?

b **Pair Work** Discuss the questions. Answer as many as possible.

1. How old was the speaker? _____
2. Who was involved? _____
3. Where did the story happen? _____
4. How was the scene described (weather, time of day)? _____
5. What happened? _____
6. How did the speaker feel? _____
7. What happened afterwards? _____
8. Did the speaker learn anything from it? _____

c Listen again and check your answers.

6a Think of two stories from your childhood. Look at the questions in Exercise 5b and write notes on a separate sheet of paper.

b Now invent another story about your childhood which is NOT true. Write notes.

c **Pair Work** Student A: Tell your three childhood stories. Answer your partner's questions. Student B: Listen to your partner's stories. Ask questions to find out more information. Guess which story is not true. Then switch roles.

Making changes

Warm Up

1   Discuss. What life changes can you see in the photos? Which are the most dramatic changes?

2a   Read the dialogs.

1. A: The sun is shining!
    B: That's **a nice change**. It's been raining all month.
2. A: Let's not go to the same restaurant tonight.
    B: Yes, **it's time for a change**.
3. A: Why did you cancel your wedding?
    B: **I had a change of heart.**
4. A: Shall we take the car?
    B: No. Let's walk **for a change**.

b   Complete the sentences so they are true for you.

1. Last week/month/year I _____. It was a nice change.
2. It was time for a change, so I _____.
3. I was planning to _____, but I had a change of heart.
4. This weekend I think I'll _____, for a change.

c   Group Work   Read your sentences. Tell the class about the most interesting changes.

Talk about cause and result CAN DO

Reading

1 Discuss. What do you know about New York City? Think about the people, the lifestyle, how New York City appears in movies, etc.

2 Read about some changes in New York City. Do any of the facts in the article surprise you?

FROM FUN CITY TO THE FORBIDDEN APPLE

NEW YORK used to be the city that never sleeps. These days it's the city that never smokes, drinks, or does anything naughty (at least, not in public). Some people say that the Big Apple has turned into the Forbidden Apple.

If you're having a picnic in Central Park and you want a glass of wine, could you have one? No way. It's illegal to drink alcohol in public. If you decided to feed the birds with the last crumbs of your sandwich, you could be arrested. It's illegal. If you went to a bar for a drink and a cigarette, that would be OK, wouldn't it? Um . . . no. You can't smoke in public in New York City.

What's going on? Why did the city that used to be so open-minded become like this? The mayor of New York was behind it all. He brought in a whole lot of new laws to stop citizens from doing what they want, when they want.

The press criticized him. And the New York police spent $100,000 on a "Don't blame us" campaign. As one New York police officer pointed out, "We raised money for the city by giving people fines for breaking some very stupid laws. It's all about money."

The result was a lot of fines for minor offences. When a tourist fell asleep on the subway, he woke up to find that the police had fined him because he had used two seats (not allowed!). One elderly couple was fined for blocking a driveway with their car. It was their own driveway.

The editor of *Vanity Fair* magazine, Graydon Carter, noted that, under New York City law, a person could keep a gun at work, but not an empty ashtray. He should know. The police came to his office and took away his ashtray.

But not all of New York's inhabitants are complaining. Marcia Dugarry, 72, said, "The city has changed for the better. If more cities had these laws, America would be a better place to live." And according to Nixon Patotkis, 38, a waiter, "I like the new laws. If people smoked in here, we'd go home smelling like cigarettes."

Crime figures show that New York now has less crime than 193 other US cities. And it's true – the Big Apple is safer, cleaner and healthier than before. But let's be honest – who visits New York for its clean streets?

3 Read the article again. Mark the statements true (*T*) or false (*F*).

____ 1. It is illegal to smoke or drink alcohol anywhere in New York.

____ 2. Eating sandwiches in the park is illegal.

____ 3. It is illegal to sleep on the subway.

____ 4. The elderly couple was fined because they parked in the wrong place.

____ 5. Some people like the new laws.

____ 6. New York is now clean and safe compared to in the past.

4 **Group Work** Discuss.

1. What is the writer's attitude to the new laws in New York? Is the article 100% serious? How do you know?

2. Do you think the laws in the article make sense? Would these laws be popular in your country?

Grammar | unreal conditional

5 Read the Active Grammar box and circle the correct choices to complete the rules (1–6).

Active Grammar

*If more cities **had** these laws, the United States **would** be a better place to live.*

*If people **smoked** in here, we'd go home smelling like cigarettes.*

1. Use the unreal conditional to describe <u>an imaginary situation</u> / <u>a real situation</u> in the present or future and its result.

2. In the *if* clause, use <u>the simple present</u> / <u>the simple past</u>.

3. In the result clause, use *would* (or *'d*) because the situation is <u>in the past</u> / <u>imaginary</u>.

4. It is possible to use a modal verb such as *could* or *might* instead of *would* if you are <u>certain</u> / <u>not sure</u> of the result.

Real conditional: *If I study hard, I will pass the test.*

Unreal conditional: *If I owned a car, I would drive to work.*

5. The <u>real conditional</u> / <u>unreal conditional</u> uses the simple present + *will*.

6. The <u>real conditional</u> / <u>unreal conditional</u> uses the simple past + *would*.

See Reference page 134

6 Make unreal conditional sentences using the verbs in parentheses.

1. If you _____ (be) a New York police officer, _____ (arrest) someone for feeding birds?

2. I _____ (not like) the new laws if I _____ (live) in New York.

3. Where _____ (go) if you _____ (want) a cigarette at work?

4. If the laws _____ (not make) money, they _____ (not exist).

5. I _____ (not be) very happy if I _____ (have to) pay a fine for using two subway seats.

6. If New York _____ (not have) these laws, tourists _____ (find) it dangerous and dirty.

7. If these laws _____ (exist) in your country, _____ (be) popular?

7 **Pair Work** Discuss. When would you do each of the situations in the box? Use the unreal conditional.

---

lie to a police officer	skip my English lesson	live in another country
go away next weekend	stay in bed until 12:00 P.M.	take a taxi
write to the government	make a long distance phone call	sing in public

---

I would go away next weekend if I didn't have to work.

Listening

8a ▶2.13 Listen to four speakers talking about things they would like to change about their city. Match the speaker to a subject.

_____ 1. Gabriel (Mexico City, Mexico)   a. noise

_____ 2. Luciana (São Paulo, Brazil)   b. buildings

_____ 3. Clive (Manchester, UK)   c. pollution

_____ 4. Min-Ji (Seoul, Korea)   d. facilities for the disabled

b Listen again. Complete the sentences below.

1. Mexico City has too many cars, _____ it's really polluted. So if I could change one thing, I'd have a law against all the traffic. I'd stop cars from going into the city center.

2. I'd improve the facilities for disabled people. People in wheelchairs have real problems _____ the roads and pavements. Even in public buildings sometimes there are no elevators _____ they can't use the rooms on the higher floors.

3. There's no peace and quiet here. All the noise and mess is _____ these students. They scream and shout every night. _____ I would make some new laws against all the noise so we could get some sleep!

4. _____ the stupid laws here, everybody builds these terrible buildings. They are really ugly, _____ the city isn't so beautiful these days. If I were mayor, I would pass a law to stop these buildings.

Speaking

9a **Pair Work** If you could propose five new laws for your city, what would they be?

b Tell the class about your laws and together choose the five best.

> If we could propose a new law, we'd stop people from driving cars into the city.

10a On a separate sheet of paper, complete the sentences.

Ex: Tokyo was expensive, so I didn't buy any souvenirs.

1. Tokyo was expensive, so . . .
2. Many travelers like Brazil because of . . .
3. Parts of Africa are very hot. Therefore, . . .
4. The pollution in many cities is caused by . . .

b **Pair Work** Compare and discuss your sentences.

Writing

11a Read the article in the Writing Bank on page 148 and do the exercises.

b Choose one of the laws you proposed in Exercise 9a. Write an article for a newspaper about the issue you'd like to change.

Vocabulary | global issues

1 **Pair Work** Discuss. What can you see in the photo? Do you think this is an effective way to initiate change? Can you think of other ways?

2 Put the words and phrases in the box in pairs. They may be opposites or have similar meanings.

Ex: *problems — solutions*

> lifestyle   famine   developed countries
> security   disease   developing countries
> crime   pollution   the environment
> ~~solutions~~   cure   standard of living
> starvation   ~~problems~~

3 Use the words and phrases from Exercise 2 to complete the sentences.

1. A lot of _____ is caused by factories and cars. This damages _____. What should be done about it?

2. Many African countries suffer from _____ when it doesn't rain for a long time. This causes _____. How can we help?

3. Do you think scientists will find the _____ for many _____, such as cancer?

4. _____, like the G8 nations, give millions of dollars every year to _____. Is this enough?

Listening

4 ▶ 2.14 Listen to two people discussing how the world has changed since they were children. Which issues in Exercise 2 do they talk about?

5 Listen again and check the phrases you hear from the How To box.

Speaking

6a **Group Work** Group 1: Write five things that have made the world better in the last 25 years. Group 2: Write five things that have made the world worse in the last 25 years.

> The standard of living has improved in most countries.

How To:	
Talk about change	
Talk about change	___ *It has gotten better/worse.*
	___ *The situation (in . . .) has improved/deteriorated.*
	___ *(Laws) have become more/less . . .*
Talk about lack of change	___ *. . . is/are still (a problem).*
	___ *. . . is/are the same.*
	___ *The situation (in . . .) hasn't changed.*
Express your attitude toward the change	___ *Luckily, . . .*
	___ *Unfortunately, . . .*
	___ *(Not) surprisingly, . . .*
	___ *Interestingly, . . .*

b Read your sentences to the other group. Respond with a more optimistic or pessimistic point of view. Use language from the How To box.

> *Yes, but unfortunately the standard of living in many countries is still poor.*

Reading

7a Look at the photos. What do you know about the Live 8 and Live Aid concerts?

b Read the article to find out/check your information.

Live Aid / Live 8
"Are you ready to start a revolution? Are you ready to change history?"

Bob Geldof

These were the words of Madonna as she walked onto the stage of the London Live 8 concert. On July 3, 2005, Live 8 concerts were held in ten cities around the globe. The idea was to highlight the problem of poverty in Africa. Hundreds of millions of people around the world watched the concerts on their televisions. But how did this all start?

The day that rock and roll really changed the world was 20 years earlier, on July 13, 1985, and all because of one man, Bob Geldof. On that day, more than a billion and a half people around the world united together to watch the biggest rock concert ever held—Live Aid.

Thirty million people were suffering in a terrible famine in sub-Saharan Africa. It was an event so completely shocking—happening on our television screens, with children dying in front of our eyes—that it moved everyone who saw it. The concert raised $220.6 million.

Live Aid was a miracle—technologically, emotionally, and politically. It is difficult now to understand what an amazing achievement it was to broadcast the first live, all-day, multi-artist concert to the whole world. In 1985 there were no cell phones and hardly any fax machines. In many countries, international phone calls usually had to be reserved, sometimes hours in advance. Computers were outside the experience of most ordinary people. Email was a future dream.

Yet surprisingly, simultaneous concerts on two continents were coordinated. Global television schedules were cleared. Live Aid started new ways of thinking and behaving—in broadcasting, in putting political pressure on governments, and in raising money. Nowadays, these have become normal as more and more charities regularly use music as an instrument for change.

Bob Geldof, the organizer of Live Aid and Live 8, saw an opportunity. He wanted to make governments and people do something important to change the terrible situation. He used what he says is "the lingua franca of the planet—not English but rock 'n' roll," and it was a fantastic success.

Live Aid was one of the first indications that we now lived in a globalized world. Interestingly, its language was music, and the message it delivered so loudly and clearly was of the need for change.

8 Pair Work Discuss.

1. Do you think Live Aid and Live 8 were successful?
2. Have you heard of or been to other charity events or concerts? What did you think of them?
3. If you organized a concert like this, what would you raise the money for? Why?
4. Do you agree that "music is an instrument for change"?

Grammar | adverbs

9 Read the Active Grammar box and circle the correct word to complete each rule. Then match these sentences from the article to the rules (1–4).

_____ a. *International phone calls **usually** had to be reserved.*

_____ b. ***Surprisingly,** simultaneous concerts on two continents were coordinated.*

_____ c. *. . . the message it delivered so **loudly and clearly** . . .*

_____ d. *It was an event so **completely** shocking . . .*

Active Grammar

An adverb is usually made by adding *-ly* to the adjective: *quiet — quietly   clear — clearly*

1. **Adverbs of manner** modify verbs. They describe the way in which something happens.

   *She talked **quietly**. Drive **carefully**!*

   Adverbs of manner usually come <u>before</u> / <u>after</u> the verb.

2. **Adverbs of frequency/probability** describe how often something happens or how probable it is.

   *She will **probably** arrive at six o'clock.*
   Adverbs of frequency usually come <u>before</u> / <u>after</u> the main verb.

3. **Adverbs of degree** make a verb weaker or stronger. They may be used for emphasis.

   *I **really** want to leave now.*

   Adverbs of degree usually come <u>before</u> / <u>after</u> the main verb.

4. Adverbs may also be used as **discourse markers** to describe your attitude.

   ***Interestingly,** she didn't call back.*

   Discourse markers often come at the <u>beginning</u> / <u>end</u> of the sentence.

See Reference page 134

10 Cross out the one adverb which cannot be used in each sentence below.

1. I will *hopefully/surprisingly/definitely* contact you as soon as we have any news.
2. *Personally/Actually/Definitely*, I am not sure that is the best plan.
3. *Hopefully/Personally/Fortunately*, Xavier will meet us at the stadium.
4. I understand the problems, but *actually/hopefully/unfortunately* I can't help.
5. The office is a terrible mess. They *obviously/definitely/hopefully* left in a hurry.
6. The school has very few books, so *not surprisingly/fortunately/obviously* the test results are poor.

Speaking

11a **Group Work** Discuss. Use adverbs.

1. Which continent has the most people?
2. What percentage of the world's people don't have enough food to eat?
3. What percentage live in houses without running water and electricity?
4. What percentage of people can read, have been to college, and own a computer?

b **SPEAKING EXCHANGE** Check the answers to the questions on page 140. Did you find any of the facts surprising, interesting, or shocking?

Speaking

1a Are you good or bad at making decisions? If you have an important decision to make, do you talk to anyone about it? Who?

b Choose three important decisions you have made in your life. Use the word box for ideas. Think about the questions below and write notes.

1. When did you make the decision?
2. Where were you?
3. Who did you talk to for advice?
4. Why did you decide to make your change?
5. Was the decision easy or difficult to make?
6. What effect did it have on your life?

start/give up a hobby	change careers
go to college	buy a home
leave your country	have a baby
start a business	leave a job or retire

c **Pair Work** Student A: Tell your partner about your three decisions. Student B: Ask your partner questions about his or her decisions to get more information. Write notes. Then switch roles.

d Tell the class about one of your partner's decisions.

Listening

2a ▶ 2.15 Listen to three people talking about important decisions they have made. What kinds of decisions do they talk about?

1 Mei Ling

2 Sarah

3 Roger

_____

_____

_____

2b Listen again. Who says these phrases? Write *Mei Ling*, *Sarah*, or *Roger*.

_____ 1. "I stopped working a year ago . . ."

_____ 2. "We . . . sold our house, left our jobs, and said good-bye to our friends."

_____ 3. "I had always dreamed of going to study in another country . . ."

_____ 4. ". . . we just fell in love with the house the moment we saw it."

_____ 5. ". . . maybe I'll change careers and start my own business."

_____ 6. "I met my fiancé, Jun, here, and we are planning to get married . . ."

Grammar | past unreal conditional

3a Read the past unreal conditional statements from the listening and answer the questions.

> **Roger:** *If I'd stayed at work, I wouldn't have spent time with Jack when he really needed me.*

1. Did Roger stay at work?

_____

2. Did he spend time with Jack?

_____

> **Mei Ling:** *I wouldn't have met Jun if I hadn't come to France!*

3. Did Mei Ling come to France?

_____

4. Did she meet Jun?

_____

Active Grammar

1. Use the past unreal conditional to talk about a <u>true</u> / <u>hypothetical</u> situation in the past.

2. Form the past unreal conditional with:

   If clause: *If* + subject + <u>past tense</u> / <u>past perfect</u>

   Main clause: subject + *would* or *wouldn't* / *would* or *wouldn't have* + past participle

   If I had stayed at work, I wouldn't have spent time with Jack.
   Past condition   Past result (hypothetical)

   I would've cooked dinner if I'd known you were coming.
   Past result (hypothetical)   Past condition

   Note: You can also use *could have* or *couldn't have*.

See Reference page 134

b Look at the Active Grammar box. Circle the correct words to complete the rules (1–2).

4 Write past unreal conditional sentences using the cues.

> **Ex:** I went on vacation to Greece. I met my husband.
> <u>*If I hadn't gone on vacation to Greece, I wouldn't*</u>
> <u>*have met my husband.*</u>

1. Taxis were very expensive. We didn't take one.

_____

2. They didn't ask anyone for directions. They got lost.

_____

3. The weather wasn't very good. We didn't enjoy the trip very much.

_____

4. It was raining. They had a car accident.

_____

5. I didn't see you when you passed me in the street. I didn't say "hello."

_____

6. I wasn't hungry. I didn't eat lunch.

_____

Pronunciation | sentence rhythm

5a ▶ 2.16 Listen to the rhythm of this sentence. Notice the stressed words.

If I'd <u>left</u> home <u>earlier</u>, I <u>wouldn't</u> have missed the <u>train</u>.

b ▶ 2.17 Listen to the sentences. Underline the stressed words.

1. If I'd known the test was today, I would have studied.

2. If I'd gone to bed earlier, I wouldn't have felt so tired.

3. If you'd asked me out to dinner, I'd have said "yes."

c Listen again and check your answers. Practice saying the sentences using the same rhythm.

Speaking

6a On a separate sheet of paper, draw two large circles. Label one circle "Now" and the other "Ten years ago." Read the questions and write short answers in the "Now" circle.

1. Where are you living?

2. Who is your closest friend?

3. What do you do?

4. How do you spend your time?

5. Are you studying?

6. Do you play any sports?

7. What music do you enjoy?

8. What are your dreams and ambitions?

b Change the questions in Exercise 6a to make questions in the past. Write short answers for these questions in the "Ten years ago" circle.

c **Pair Work** Show your circles to your partner. Talk about how much your life has changed in the past ten years. Ask questions to find out as much information as possible.

Writing

7 Write a paragraph describing an important turning point in your life and the effect this had. Think about what happened before and after the event and how things might have been different if it hadn't happened.

get married?

back to college?

change job?

sell house?

SOLD

Review

1 Rewrite the following using *if* sentences with *would*.

> **Ex:** I am too old. I can't learn to play handball. (If) _*If I was/were younger, I would learn to play handball.*_

1. She doesn't have Dave's number. She wants to call him. (If) _____
2. I can't go out. I have a test tomorrow. (I'd) _____
3. We want to buy a new car. We don't have enough money right now. (If) _____
4. There isn't time. They can't see the show. (They'd) _____
5. I don't have a choice. I want to live in the city. (If) _____

2 Write questions to complete the dialogs using the verbs in parentheses. Use the conditional (real or unreal).

> **Ex: A:** What (do) _*would you do if you lost your passport?*_
>
> **B:** Lost my passport? I'd go to the embassy.

1. **A:** How (feel) _____
   B: Got the job? I'd be extremely happy!
2. **A:** Which (buy) _____
   B: If I had the choice? I'd buy the house on the hill.
3. **A:** What (do) _____
   B: A train delay? I'll take a taxi.
4. **A:** Where (go) _____
   B: No rooms? We'll find a different hotel.
5. **A:** How (celebrate) _____
   B: Got a raise? I'd have a big party.

3 Make adverbs from the words in parentheses. Write the adverb in one of the blanks to complete each sentence.

> **Ex:** _*Hopefully*_ we will see _____ them at the party. (hopeful)

1. I _____ go _____ to the supermarket on Saturdays. (usual)
2. Susana is so _____ busy that I _____ ever see her anymore. (hard)
3. Steve _____ drives when we _____ go on long trips. (normal)
4. I exercise _____ in _____ the gym. (regular)
5. We _____ don't _____ want to damage the relationship. (certain)

4 Put the verbs into the correct form to make past unreal conditional sentences.

> **Ex:** If she _*had asked*_ (ask) me to help her, we _*would have finished*_ (finish) the job yesterday.

1. If I _____ (know) you were coming, I _____ (cook) more pasta.
2. If Ken _____ (leave) five minutes earlier this morning, he _____ (not miss) the train.
3. If you _____ (tell) me you needed to get up early, I _____ (wake) you.
4. If she _____ (see) the mess, she _____ (be) angry.
5. If I _____ (not drink) that coffee, I _____ (fall asleep) during the movie.

Communication | discuss your feelings about change

5 **Pair Work** Discuss. If you could change one thing in your life, what would you like to change? Use the photos for ideas.

> *I'd like to have a bigger apartment so that I could invite my friends to stay.*

6a **SPEAKING EXCHANGE** Student A: Add two more questions to the questionnaire below. Student B: Add two more questions to the questionnaire on page 142.

b **Pair Work** Ask your partner the questions. Then ask follow-up questions to get more information. Circle the answers your partner gives you.

Are you ready FOR CHANGE?

1. Do you like to go to new places and meet new people?	Yes/No
2. Do you regularly watch the same television shows every week?	Yes/No
3. Do you go to the same place on vacation every year?	Yes/No
4. Do you hope to have the same job for your whole life?	Yes/No
5. Do you usually go out with the same group of people?	Yes/No
6. Can you imagine living in many different places?	Yes/No
7. (your own question) _____	Yes/No
8. (your own question) _____	Yes/No

c Did your partner answer "yes" to more than half the questions? Do you think your partner likes change? Tell the class.

UNIT 9
On the job

Warm Up

1 **Pair Work** Discuss. Describe the work environments in the photos. What are the pros and cons of working in each place?

2 Complete the sentences with a word or phrase from the box.

> promoted   flexible   self-employed
> overtime   raise   dress code

1. One advantage of being _____ is that you are your own boss and you can set your own hours.
2. I have _____ hours—some days I start at 8:00 A.M. and other days I start at 9:00.
3. Last week my husband worked his usual 40 hours but also had to work 5 hours of _____ .
4. Victor got a _____ last week. His wages went up from $12 an hour to $14.
5. I'm an assistant manager right now. I hope to be _____ to manager next year.
6. We have a strict _____ in my office. Everyone has to wear a suit.

Reading

1 **Pair Work** Which workers typically do these things? Discuss.

> wear uniforms   set salaries   do the photocopying   set working hours
> fix equipment   type letters   meet guests in reception   evaluate workers

> *Secretaries often type letters.*

2a Read the introduction to the article. Who is Ricardo Semler? What problem did he have?

At 21, Ricardo Semler became the boss of his father's business in Brazil, Semco, which sold parts for ships.

Semler junior worked like a madman from 7:30 A.M. until midnight every day. One afternoon, while touring a factory in New York, he collapsed. The doctor who treated him said, "There's nothing wrong with you. Yet. But if you continue like this, you'll find a new home in our hospital." Semler got the message. He changed the way he worked. In fact, he changed the way his employees worked, too.

b What changes do you think Semler made? Discuss with other students and write a list. Read the rest of the article to find out.

" Everyone at Semco, even top managers, meets guests in reception, does the photocopying, sends faxes, types letters, and dials the phone. "

Semler let his workers take more responsibility so that they would be the ones worrying when things went wrong. He allowed them to set their own salaries, and he cut all the jobs he thought were unnecessary, like receptionists and secretaries. This saved money and brought more equality to the company. "Everyone at Semco, even top managers, meets guests in reception, does the photocopying, sends faxes, types letters, and dials the phone."

He completely reorganized the office: Instead of walls, they have plants at Semco, so bosses can't shut themselves away from everyone else. And the workers are free to decorate their workspace as they want. There is no dress code at Semco—some people wear suits, and others wear T-shirts.

Semco has flexible working hours; the employees decide when they need to arrive at work. The employees also evaluate their bosses twice a year. In addition, Semco lets its workers use the company's machines for their own projects, and makes them take at least 30 vacation days per year.

It sounds perfect, but does it work? The answer is in the numbers: In the last six years, Semco's revenues have gone from $35 million to $212 million. The company has grown from 800 employees to 3,000. Why?

Semler says it's because of "peer pressure." Peer pressure makes everyone work hard for everyone else. If someone isn't doing his or her job, the other workers will not allow the situation to continue. In other words, Ricardo Semler treats his workers like adults and expects them to act like adults. And they do.

3 Read the article again and answer the questions.

1. What do employees at Semco do that they probably wouldn't do in other companies?
2. How do Semco and its staff look different from other companies?
3. How does Semco show that it trusts its workers?
4. Do Semco's methods work? How do we know?
5. What is "peer pressure" and why is it important at Semco?

4 **Group Work** Discuss.

1. What do you think of Semco's policies? Would you like to work at Semco?
2. Would any of the "rules" at Semco be possible where you work or in your country? Why or why not?

> I think some of the policies are good. For example, . . .

Grammar | *make/let/allow*

5a Read the example sentences and complete the Active Grammar box with *make*, *let*, or *allow*.

Active Grammar

*Semco **lets** its workers use the company's machines.*

*Semco **makes** the workers take vacations.*

*Semler **allowed** the workers to set their own salaries.*

Meaning

1. _____ and _____ mean give permission to do something.
2. _____ means force to do something.

Form

3. _____ + person + verb (force to do)
4. _____ + person + verb (give permission to do)
5. _____ + person + *to* + verb (give permission to do)

Use

6. Don't use *let* in the passive voice.

See Reference page 135

b Find other examples of *make*, *let,* and *allow* in the article on page 104.

6 Complete the sentences with the correct form of *make, let,* or *(not) allow(ed)*.

1. My last employers were really easygoing. They _____ us go home early on Fridays.
2. The employees are _____ to take one month off each year.
3. Dan's music was annoying his co-workers. So the boss _____ him turn it down.
4. He was really strict with the workers. He _____ them work on weekends.
5. It's my favorite airline. They _____ young children to fly for free.
6. I don't like going to customer service. They _____ you wait forever before the manager sees you.
7. Our boss was very relaxed. She _____ us take long breaks.

Listening

7a ▶ 2.18 Listen to the presentation of a new business and answer the questions.

1. What type of business is it?
2. What is special about this business?
3. What will the chefs be allowed to do?
4. How many employees will they have?
5. What is the name of the business?

b Listen again and take notes. Write the phrases the speaker uses to start and finish her presentation.

Speaking

8a **Pair Work** You are going to start a new company. Decide:

1. what your company does.
2. the company's name.
3. how big it is.
4. where it is based.

b Think about how you will treat your employees. Will you:

1. let them work flexible hours?
2. make them work long hours and overtime?
3. let them take a lot of responsibility? How?
4. make them follow a dress code?

9a Write notes in the Company Profile.

⚛ COMPANY PROFILE

Company name: _____

Address: _____

Type of business: _____

_____

Customer profile: _____

_____

Future plans: _____

_____

Number of employees: _____

Notes for employees: _____

_____

_____

_____

_____

Vacation days: _____

_____

b **Group Work** Present your ideas to the rest of the class. Use the language in the How To box. Other students take notes and ask questions.

c Discuss which company you would want to work for. Explain why.

How To:

Present ideas to a group	
Welcome	*Hello everyone.* *Good morning/afternoon/evening.*
Introducing the topic	*I'd like to tell you about . . .* *First, I'm going to talk about . . .* *Second, I'll talk about . . .*
Emphasizing	*The main point is . . .* *The most important thing is . . .*
Conclusion	*In conclusion, . . .* *To wrap up, . . .*
Final comments	*Thank you for listening.* *Are there any questions?*

Listening

1   Discuss. What are some things good bosses do?
What are some things bad bosses do?

> *Good bosses understand their employees' feelings.*

2   ▶ 2.19   Listen to people talk about their managers.
What does each speaker think about his or her boss?
Write notes in the chart.

Speaker 1	
Speaker 2	
Speaker 3	
Speaker 4	

Vocabulary | *-ing/-ed* adjectives

3   Look at the examples and circle the correct word or phrase to complete the rules.

I am frightened.   *It is frightening.*

  1. Use *-ed* adjectives to talk about <u>*feelings/situations that cause feelings*</u>.

  2. Use *-ing* adjectives to talk about <u>*feelings/situations that cause feelings*</u>.

4   Circle the correct adjective to complete each sentence.

  1. I think English grammar is a little <u>*confused/confusing*</u>.

  2. I'm <u>*exhausted/exhausting*</u>. I just jogged around the park.

  3. Can we stop talking about politics? It's very <u>*bored/boring*</u>.

  4. I'm not watching that horror movie. It's too <u>*frightened/frightening*</u>.

  5. I hate getting up early every day. It's so
    <u>*tired/tiring*</u>.

  6. I don't watch the news on television
    because I find it too <u>*depressed/depressing*</u>.

  7. I don't walk alone at night. I'm too
    <u>*frightened/frightening*</u>.

  8. I love sitting in a café and reading the
    newspaper in the morning. It's very
    <u>*relaxed/relaxing*</u>.

  9. I'm going to watch the World Cup final
    tonight. I'm so <u>*excited/exciting*</u>!

Reading

5 **Pair Work** Look at the title of the story and the picture. What do you think the story is about? Discuss. Then read the story.

> *I think the story is about . . .*

The Engineer and the Manager

A man flying in a hot air balloon realized he was lost. He started to come down until he could see a man on the ground who might hear him. "Excuse me," he shouted. "Can you help me? I promised my friend I would meet him a half hour ago, but I don't know where I am, or where I am going."

The man below responded: "Yes. You are in a hot air balloon, approximately 30 feet above this field. You are between 40 and 42 degrees North Latitude, and between 58 and 60 degrees West Longitude."

"You must be an engineer," responded the balloonist. "I am," the man replied. "How did you know?" "Well," said the balloonist, "everything you have told me is technically correct, but I have no idea what to do with this information, and the fact is I am still lost."

Whereupon the man on the ground responded, "You must be a manager." "I am," replied the balloonist, "but how did you know?" "Well," said the man, "you don't know where you are, or where you're going. You've made a promise which you can't keep, and you expect me to solve your problem. The fact is you are in the exact same position you were before we met, but now it's my fault."

Grammar | reported speech: statements

6 Match the sentences to what the people actually said (a–c) in the story.

_____ 1. *The manager asked if the engineer could help him.*

_____ 2. *The manager said (that) he didn't know where he was going.*

_____ 3. *The manager told the engineer (that) he was still lost.*

a. "I am still lost."

b. "Can you help me?"

c. "I don't know where I am going."

7 Read the example sentences in the Active Grammar box. Circle the correct choices to complete the rules.

Active Grammar

Reported speech usually uses *say* or *tell*. If you use the verb <u>*say*</u> / <u>*tell*</u>, you must mention the listener. When you report speech, you usually <u>change</u> / <u>don't change</u> the tense one step back.

*He **said** (that)/**told me** (that) he was still lost.*

Direct speech	Reported speech
"I'll help you."	He **said** he **would**/**could help** me.
"Carly is in a meeting."	She **told me** Carly **was** in a meeting.
"I am going to meet Marc."	He **said** he **was going to meet** Marc.
"Tom has been late every day."	He **told me** Tom **had been** late every day.
"He didn't buy it yesterday."	She **told me** he **hadn't bought** it the day before.

See Reference page 135

8 On a separate sheet of paper, change the sentences to reported speech.

1. "I'm the new technician." He said . . .

2. "I'll be back tomorrow." Mom said . . .

3. "I've been stuck in traffic." Mara told us . . .

4. "He won't be away for long." She said . . .

5. "I'll carry your bag for you." He said . . .

6. "We're going on vacation next week." They told me . . .

7. "I went shopping yesterday." He told us . . .

8. "I'm feeling better." She told him . . .

Listening

9 ▶2.20 Listen to the interview and circle the correct choice to complete each sentence.

1. He says that _____ .
   a. he has a lot of problems
   b. he likes talking about his problems
   c. people like talking to him about their problems

2. He tells her that _____ .
   a. he works hard b. he hardly works c. he doesn't like work

3. He says that _____ .
   a. he is organized b. he is disorganized c. he likes organizing things

4. He tells her that _____ .
   a. he doesn't panic b. he often panics c. he isn't a calm person

5. He says that _____ .
   a. he finds working on his own difficult b. he likes working with people
   c. he doesn't like to work from home

Grammar | reported speech: questions

10 Read the Active Grammar box and circle the correct choices to complete the rules (1–2).

11 Write the questions in reported speech. Start with "She asked me . . .".
   1. Are you good at organizing people?
   2. Do you enjoy working as part of a team?
   3. What do you do when your ideas don't work?
   4. Do you listen to other people's advice?
   5. What do you do when you have too much work?
   6. What time do you normally get to work?

Active Grammar

Direct question	Reported question
"Do you like working in an office?"	I **asked** her **if/whether** she liked working in an office.
"What is your name?"	I **asked** her what her name was.

1. Use <u>say</u> / <u>tell</u> / <u>ask</u> to report questions.
2. Use *if* or *whether* to report <u>yes/no</u> / <u>information</u> questions.

See Reference page 135

12 Complete the sentences with *said*, *told*, or *asked*. There may be more than one correct answer.
   1. Anna _____ me that she would be back by five o'clock.
   2. Mara _____ me to turn the computer off when I left the office.
   3. My brother _____ me to wait for him at the station.
   4. The driver _____ that he was feeling sick.
   5. The sales clerk _____ if we needed help.
   6. Her boss _____ her that she could take the afternoon off.

Speaking

13a Write five questions to ask your partner to find out if he or she would make a good manager.
   Ex: *Do you like . . . ? Are you good at . . . ? What . . . ? Can you . . . ? Do you . . . ?*

b **Pair Work** Interview your partner. Report your partner's answers back to the class.

> *I asked Maria if she preferred working on her own*
> *or as part of a team, and she told me she likes . . .*

Reading

1 **Pair Work** Discuss. What's the most unusual job you've ever had? What did you have to do?

2 Read the interviews. Summarize each person's job in one sentence.

WHAT'S THE MOST UNUSUAL JOB YOU'VE EVER HAD?

Bruno Campisi — Plane Repossessor, Chicago, USA
My most unusual job was as an airplane repo man for a large bank. If people couldn't pay for the planes they had bought, I **had to take** the plane back from them. The upside: I **could fly** airplanes. The downside: I **had to deal with** dangerous, angry owners. I **wasn't allowed to carry** a gun, but sometimes the owners had guns. On my last job, I hurt my leg and **couldn't run** fast any more. I **had to change** to a less active career. I'm a computer technician now!

Ram Bhatnagar — Monkey Catcher, Delhi, India
The most unusual job I've ever had was also the most difficult! To get the job of monkey catcher, I **didn't have to** learn any new skills. I just **had to be** an excellent tree climber and physically fit. Since Hindus consider monkeys sacred, I **couldn't** hurt or kill them. I **had to chase** them through city streets, on rooftops, or in tunnels and carefully grab them and wrestle them into cages. With all the bites and scratches, I **couldn't do** this job for more than a month. I caught a total of 250 monkeys. The pay was really good: 450 rupees per monkey. I'm living off that money now and looking for less dangerous work.

Daniela Garcia — Laughter Therapist, Valencia, Venezuela
My most unusual job was as a laughter therapist for cancer patients at a hospital. Therapists help people deal with their problems. As a laughter therapist, I **had to help** people see the funny side of life. This wasn't always easy with cancer patients. I used different techniques for encouraging laughter. In one exercise, patients **had to practice** laughter sounds like "hee-hee," "ha-ha," and "ho-ho," which often turned into laughter. Or they **had to communicate** using these laughing sounds instead of words. The goal was for everyone to end up laughing. **I couldn't force** people to laugh, but it was rewarding when the therapy worked. Now I'm a general therapist, but I still use laughter with many of my patients.

Kumiko Hisakawa — Professional Sleeper, Yokohama, Japan
As a student, I was always tired and poor. So I found a way to get rest and make a lot of money — sleep studies. I often **had to sleep** at a hospital or research facility one night or more. Usually I **was allowed** to bring my own pillow and pajamas. I also **had to take** a variety of tests. But it paid very well. There was one particularly strange job that I did at an art museum. I **had to take** a sleeping pill and fall asleep as part of a living exhibit. I don't sleep professionally any more — I am an ER physician. But professional sleeping helped me pay for medical school!

3 **Pair Work** Discuss. Would you be interested in any of the jobs in the interviews? Which job could you never do? Why not?

4 Mark each statement true (*T*), false (*F*), or No Information (*NI*).

____ 1. Ram was a monkey catcher for several months.

____ 2. Daniela's job was to try to make patients laugh.

____ 3. It is against Hindu religion to kill monkeys.

____ 4. Bruno traveled with a gun for protection.

____ 5. Kumiko still sleeps professionally sometimes.

____ 6. Bruno's job as a repossessor paid a lot of money.

____ 7. Laughter therapy will work on anyone.

____ 8. Kumiko was part of an art exhibit.

Grammar | past obligation/permission

5 Look at the example sentences in the Active Grammar box and circle the correct choices to complete the rules (1–2).

Active Grammar

necessary (in the past)
*I **had to sleep** at a hospital.*

not necessary (in the past)
*I **didn't have to learn** any new skills.*

OK/permitted (in the past)
*I **was allowed to bring** my own pillow and pajamas.*
*I **could** fly airplanes.*

not OK/not permitted (in the past)
*I **wasn't allowed to carry** a gun.*
*I **couldn't** force people to laugh.*

1. *Could/couldn't* are followed by the infinitive / base form .

2. *Had to/didn't have to* and *was(n't)/were(n't) allowed to* are followed by the gerund / base form .

See Reference page 135

6 Complete the sentences with modal verbs from the Active Grammar box. There may be more than one answer.

Ex: Martin wasn't in the office, so I _had to_____ call him on his cell phone.

1. When I was in school, we _____ run inside the building.

2. In my last job, we _____ work from home two days a week.

3. Luckily, we had our passports with us, so we _____ go back to the hotel to get them.

4. We _____ smoke in the restaurant, so we _____ go outside.

5. I stayed up all night because I _____ finish my assignment by today.

6. As a child, I was _____ watch TV for an hour a day.

7. The flight was delayed, but we _____ wait very long.

7a Correct the mistakes in the following sentences.

1. I wasn't be allowed to stay out late.

2. We could to eat chocolate all day long.

3. Did you were allowed to buy new clothes?

4. We didn't allowed to watch television.

5. I couldn't to use the telephone because it was too expensive.

6. We always did have to finish our food.

7. We didn't had to help with the housework.

8. We had to practicing very hard.

b **Pair Work** Discuss. Are the corrected sentences in Exercise 7a true for you when you were a child?

> *When I was a child, I could use the telephone, but I wasn't allowed to talk for very long.*

Vocabulary | job skills and responsibilities

8 Match the job skills and responsibilities with the definitions.

Job skills and responsibilities	Definitions
____ 1. dealing with people	a. planning or arranging activities
____ 2. solving problems	b. giving jobs to others to do
____ 3. persuading people	c. working at unusual times, such as very early or late
____ 4. making decisions	d. deciding which jobs are more/less important
____ 5. organizing	e. getting people to do things they don't want to do
____ 6. delegating	f. working with others
____ 7. prioritizing	g. working in stressful situations
____ 8. working under pressure	h. finding answers to difficult situations
____ 9. working accurately	i. making choices
____ 10. working irregular hours	j. not making mistakes

Listening

9a ▶ 2.21 Listen to four people talking about their jobs. What type of job does each person talk about? Match the speakers (1–4) with the photos (A–D).

____ Speaker 1

____ Speaker 2

____ Speaker 3

____ Speaker 4

b **Pair Work** Listen again. What job skills or responsibilities are mentioned for each job?

A

B

C

Speaking

10a Think about how to describe your job or a job that you would like to have in the future. Write notes on a separate sheet of paper. Use vocabulary from Exercise 8.

> Think about location, main tasks, job requirements, pros and cons, etc.

b **Pair Work** Describe your job. Ask questions about your partner's job.

> Do you have to work under pressure?

> Yes, sometimes.

D

Review

1 Complete the letter with the words from the box.

> let   lets   ~~allowed~~
> them   don't   make

2 On a separate sheet of paper, change the statements and questions to reported speech.

> **Ex:** "What's your name?" He asked me *what my name was.*

1. "I've made a lot of new friends." He told me he . . .
2. "I'll call you tomorrow." She said she . . .
3. "I went to a great presentation this morning." She said she . . .
4. "I live in an apartment with three other students." He told me he . . .
5. "Where can I change some money?" He asked . . .
6. "Have you been here before?" She asked . . .
7. "Will you water my plants for me?" She asked . . .
8. "Did you see a movie last night?" They asked if we . . .
9. "Are you meeting anyone here?" He asked . . .

Mount Airy Summer Camp

Dear Ms. Salvagnoni,

In reply to your questions, let me assure you that the children are not ___*allowed*___ (1.) to leave the camp without an adult. We _____ (2.) the children play outside from 3:00 P.M. to 5:00 P.M., though we never _____ (3.) the children do any activity that they don't want to do. We _____ (4.) allow children to bring computer games to the camp, though the camp manager _____ (5.) students use the Internet. We also let _____ (6.) call home free of charge twice a week. I hope this answers your questions.

Yours sincerely,

Paula Burholt

---

3 Complete the sentences with *had to*, *didn't have to*, *could*, *couldn't*, *were allowed*, or *weren't allowed*.

> Working from home has changed my life. Before, I _____ *had to* _____ (1.) be in my office by 9 A.M., but now I work when I want to, and I can wear whatever I like. I _____ (2.) wear pajamas in the office! In fact, we _____ (3.) wear suits, which I hated. Another good thing is that I don't have to commute. Before, I never got home before 8:00, because we _____ (4.) to leave the office before 6:00. On the other hand, working at home is a little lonely. Also, I have to pay for computer software. Before, I _____ (5.) buy anything. And if I have a computer problem, I have to fix it. Before, I _____ (6.) ask the IT technician to do it.

4 Circle the correct choice to complete each sentence.

> **Ex:** We're good at (solving)/organizing problems.

1. My job can be very *bored/tired/tiring*.
2. When I'm busy, I always *prioritize/delegate/persuade* some of the work to my co-workers.
3. Eventually, we *prioritized/persuaded/organized* the boss to give us a raise.
4. It was very *boring/annoyed/annoying* when my computer stopped working.
5. You need to work *accurate/irregular/quick* hours in this job.
6. I read my manager's email, but I was *confused/confusing/relaxing*. I didn't understand her instructions.

Communication | prepare for a job interview

5 Look at the job listings. Choose the job you would most like to apply for. List the job requirements. Then list the reasons why you would be a good choice for the job.

GRAPHIC DESIGNER

ATG GROUP is a fast-growing import company. We are currently looking for a GRAPHIC DESIGNER for a busy design department. We require a dynamic, highly motivated individual with at least two years' experience. You must have knowledge of a range of software applications and digital media, including photography. You need to be able to work under pressure, be a good communicator, and have a flexible approach to work.

Wanted

FISHES Restaurant and Bar. Part-time exp. bar and restaurant service staff required. Pays well. Must be vibrant, confident, and smart.

FISHES Restaurant and Bar

Looking for a new start? Working abroad? Time for a change?

- Average working day: 9 to 5:30, 5 days per week. No experience required—full training will be given. Travel and work in a team dealing with the public. Fantastic long-term career and job prospects.

News editor

We are a leading international newspaper group. We are looking for new journalists to join our friendly team. If you're an experienced editor looking for a new challenge, or a journalist with previous experience, we would like to hear from you. Fluency in foreign languages an advantage.

Marketing Manager

We are a major supplier of educational products to primary and secondary schools. The successful applicant needs experience in managing advertising and marketing campaigns and in reporting on the results. Ability to read data and manage people is vital.

6 **Pair Work** Tell a partner which job you chose. Write a list of interview questions to ask your partner about his or her job. Then interview your partner. Use your lists to ask and answer questions.

> *What software can you use?*   *I can use Photoshop and . . .*

Warm Up

1a Look at the photos. What do you know about these famous memorials?

b Circle the correct words or phrases to complete the sentences.
1. The Taj Mahal was built by Emperor Shah Jahan *in memory of/to miss* his beloved wife.
2. The Lincoln Memorial was built so that we'd never *lose/forget* President Lincoln and his work.
3. This memorial was placed here to *remind us to/remind us of* John Lennon's vision of a peaceful world.
4. This statue was created to *remember/remind* Hachikó, a faithful dog that waited for its owner at a Tokyo train station, for many years after its owner died.

2 What's the difference in meaning between the following pairs?
1. lose/forget   2. remind me to/remind me of   3. remember/remind

3 **Pair Work** Are there any memorials in your country? Who built them and why?

Reading

1a Look at the words and pictures (A–C) from three stories about memory. What do you think is happening in each story?

A   LOST, MEMORY, DOCUMENTS

B   UNCONSCIOUS, FORGOTTEN, GIRLFRIEND

C   REMEMBER, FACTS, SECRET

b Read the stories below and match the pictures to the stories.

Story 1

Colin Brown, 29, fell unconscious after hitting his head in a bicycling accident. When he regained consciousness in the hospital two days later, he had forgotten four years of his life. Unfortunately, this included his three-year relationship with Lydia Davis, his girlfriend.

Lydia says Colin didn't even recognize her when she visited him in the hospital. "He would tell me to leave and would shout for the nurse to take me away," she said.

But Lydia refused to give up. "We went to the movies, started eating out, and talked about what we liked to do."

Story 2

In 1999 a man walked into a hospital in Sydney, Australia. He had lost all his documents and was suffering from a terrible headache. He'd also lost his memory. Despite police investigations and television appeals, no one was able to identify him.

He said, "It is as though I don't exist. My life is senseless."

The man, who was named "Mr. Nobody" by the media, couldn't get a passport, and he spent his time at home watching videos or reading in the library. Mr. Nobody was obviously an educated man. He played the piano and spoke French and Italian. But what he really wanted was to find out who he was.

Story 3

S. was a journalist for a Moscow newspaper in the 1920s. He would never take notes, but his reports were always full of perfectly remembered facts. He was so good that his editor sent him to a psychologist, a man named Luria. Luria discovered that S. could memorize, in a few minutes, long lists of numbers and remember them for weeks. Nobody knew how he did it.

Thirty years after they first met, Luria tested S. and S. could still remember all the numbers perfectly. Amazed, Luria asked him how he managed to do it. He wanted to discover the secret of S.'s amazing memory.

2 Read the stories again and mark the sentences true (*T*) or false (*F*).

___ 1. Colin forgot everything about his life.

___ 2. Lydia tried to continue their relationship.

___ 3. Mr. Nobody knew nothing about his identity.

___ 4. Mr. Nobody was good at several things.

___ 5. S. went to see Luria to improve his memory.

___ 6. Luria tested S.'s memory every year for 30 years.

Speaking

3a **SPEAKING EXCHANGE** Write titles and your own short endings for the stories. Share them with other groups.

b Read the real endings on page 141. Which story is the most interesting?

Listening

4a **Pair Work** What are you good at remembering? What do you sometimes forget?

b ▶2.22 Listen to Alicia and Jack talking about things they remember or forget. What do they mention?

c Listen again and complete the sentences.

1. **Alicia:** Do you have a good memory?

   Jack: I wish I _____!

2. **Jack:** I write them all down on my calendar. I wish I _____ have to, but . . .

3. **Alicia:** I wish I _____ things like writers' names or the names of songs.

Grammar | *I wish/if only*

5 Read the example sentences (1–6) in the Active Grammar box. Match the examples with the rules (a–f).

> ### Active Grammar
>
> ____ 1. *He wishes he had a sister.*
>
> ____ 2. *I wish I were taller.*
>
> ____ 3. *I wish they would be quiet.*
>
> ____ 4. *She wishes she could drive.*
>
> ____ 5. *They wish they had gone to bed early last night.*
>
> ____ 6. *If only I could sing.*
>
> a. Don't use *was* after *wish*; use *were*.
>
> b. Use *If only* instead of *wish* when you want the meaning to be a little stronger.
>
> c. Use *wish + could* when you want to talk about ability.
>
> d. Use *wish + would* when you want someone or something to change.
>
> e. Use *wish +* the past perfect to talk about imaginary things we wanted to be true in the past.
>
> f. Use *wish +* the simple past to talk about imaginary things we would like to be true in the present.

See Reference page 136

6 Complete the second sentence in each pair so that the meaning is the same as the meaning in the first sentence.

Ex: I'm hungry and I didn't eat earlier. I wish _I had eaten_____ earlier.

1. I'm bad at math. I wish _____ better at math.

2. You're late again. I wish _____ arrive on time!

3. We went to a museum yesterday and we were so bored. I wish _____ gone there.

4. I'd love to be a good dancer, but I can't dance. If only _____ dance.

5. I'm lonely because I don't have enough friends. I wish _____ more friends.

6. Steve is tired because he went to bed late. He wishes _____ to bed earlier.

7. My bus is stuck in traffic and I'm going to be late for my flight. If only _____ taken an earlier bus.

7 **Pair Work** Choose five skills from the box you wish you had. Explain your choices.

> see the future
> become invisible
> fly like a bird
> travel in time
>
> swim like a fish
> be incredibly strong
> read people's thoughts
> remember everything you read

> *I wish I could fly like a bird, because I would travel all over the world for free!*

Reading

8a **Pair Work** Look at some beliefs about wish-making from different countries. Some are true and others have been invented. Guess which are true. Explain your reasons.

1. **Brazil:** Tie a ribbon around your wrist using three knots. Make a wish for each knot. When the ribbon falls off, your three wishes will come true.

2. **Japan:** Fold a thousand origami paper cranes and make a wish. A crane will make this wish come true!

3. **Russia:** Stand between two people with the same name. If you make a wish, it will come true.

4. **Cuba:** As the clock strikes 12:00 midnight on New Year's, quickly eat 12 grapes and make a wish for each one. If you finish before 12:01 A.M., your wishes will come true.

5. **Kenya:** A zebra is a symbol of good luck. If you see a herd of zebras running, make a wish. They will carry your wish, and it will come true.

6. **Mexico:** If you get salt water from the ocean in your mouth, quickly make a wish before the salty taste disappears and you'll get your wish.

7. **Canada:** Make a wish before going through a tunnel or over a bridge, and then hold your breath. If you cross without taking a breath, your wish will come true.

8. **China:** If you see yourself reflected in a river, make a wish. If you see someone else reflected, quickly look away or you will have bad luck.

b ▶2.23 Listen and check your answers. Did any of the answers surprise you?

Speaking

9 **Group Work** Discuss.

1. Do you know any traditional beliefs about wish-making? Do you believe in any of them?
2. What kinds of things have you wished for? Did your wishes come true?

Discuss personal qualities— talk about past events

CAN DO ✓

GRAMMAR review of past tenses

Listening

1 **Pair Work** What do you know about the women in the photos?

Frida Kahlo

Mother Teresa

Marilyn Monroe

Marie Curie

2a ▶2.24 Listen. Why are the women memorable?

b Listen again and complete the notes.

1. Frida Kahlo was famous for her amazing and unusual _____.
2. Mother Teresa helped the sick in India. Her charities are active in more than _____ countries.
3. Marie Curie worked with her _____ and won the Nobel Prize in 1903 and _____.
4. Marilyn Monroe starred in _____ films and is remembered for her _____.

Vocabulary | personal qualities

3a Match the words in **bold** with the words and phrases in the box.

> very intelligent   spent all her time   very good at (something)
> played a part in   never stopped trying   made people want to (do something)

1. Marilyn Monroe was a **talented** actress. _____
2. Mother Teresa **dedicated her life** to helping the sick. _____
3. Frida Kahlo was **determined** to survive and made a remarkable recovery. _____
4. Marie Curie was a **brilliant** scientist. _____
5. Frida Kahlo was **involved in** a serious accident. _____
6. Mother Teresa **inspired** many people to start caring for others. _____

b Complete the sentences with a word or phrase in **bold** from Exercise 3a.

1. The pain Frida Kahlo experienced in her life _____ her to explore these themes in her art.
2. Mother Teresa was _____ charity work in India and saved thousands of lives.
3. Marilyn Monroe was _____ to become a movie star.
4. Marie Curie _____ to science.

4 **Pair Work** Can you think of any other memorable people of the 20th century? Choose two people and discuss their personal qualities. Use the vocabulary.

Reading

5 Read about another memorable woman of the 20th century. Guess the answers and follow the instructions.

The Making of Chanel

1 Coco Chanel was born in a home for poor people in Saumur, France, on August 19, 1883, and was christened Gabrielle. Her mother died when she was just six years old. This left her father with Gabrielle and four other young children. What happened next?

a. The father brought them up alone.

b. The children became film stars.

c. The father sent them away.

Read 5 to find out ⟩⟩

7 She had worked for a short time as a nurse in World War I, but during World War II she went to Switzerland. She returned to France in 1953 and dressed many Hollywood stars such as Elizabeth Taylor and Katharine Hepburn. What happened next?

a. She acted in a film about her life.

b. She died in the 1970s.

c. She moved to the West Indies.

⟨⟨ **Read 4 to find out**

5 He sent them away to grow up with relatives. In her early 20s, while she was working as a singer in cafés, Gabrielle met two wealthy men, one a soldier, the other an Englishman named Arthur Capel. What did the men do?

a. They shot each other because they loved her.

b. They helped her start a clothes business.

c. They paid for her to travel around the world.

Read 3 to find out ⟩⟩

3 With the men's money and contacts, she opened a hat store in 1913. She soon expanded her business to include clothes and opened a fashion store at 31 rue Cambon, Paris. What happened next?

a. She married a politician.

b. She became a singer.

c. She designed clothes for women.

⟨⟨ **Read 6 to find out**

4 She was still working up until her death on January 10, 1971, when her fashion empire brought in over $160 million a year. Before that, in 1969, Katharine Hepburn had starred in a Broadway musical about her life. She is considered one of the most influential fashion designers of the 20th century.

THE END

6 She began to design clothes for women. She said, "Most women dress for men and want to be admired. But they must also be able to move, to get into a car. Clothes must have a natural shape." What was her other famous product?

a. Shoes.

b. Perfume.

c. Furniture.

Read 2 to find out ⟩⟩

2 In the early 1920s she introduced Chanel No. 5, which became one of the world's favorite perfumes. Throughout the 1920s and '30s her clothes were becoming more and more popular. But then, in 1939, World War II began. What happened to her?

a. She moved to Switzerland.

b. She designed uniforms for soldiers.

c. She worked as a nurse.

Read 7 to find out ↑

6 **Pair Work** Retell Coco Chanel's story using the numbers and dates in the box.

August 19, 1883	six years old	two men	1913	No. 5	January 10, 1971
1920s and 1930s	31 rue Cambon	$160 million	1953	1939	

Grammar | review of past tenses

7a Look at the Active Grammar box and complete the rules. Write *past perfect*, *past continuous*, or *simple past*.

Active Grammar

1. Use the _____ to describe the main events of a story in the past.

2. Use the _____ to describe things that happened before the main events in the past.

3. Use the _____ to describe actions that were already in progress when the main events happened.

4. The _____ and the _____ are often used together when one action was in progress and the other action happened suddenly.
   He **was sleeping** when the storm **began**.

5. The _____ and the _____ are often used together to make it clear which action happened before another action in the past.
   *I **felt** ill because I **had eaten** bad food.*

See Reference page 136

b Find examples of the tenses above in the Reading on page 120.

8 Read about Gianni Versace. Put the verbs in parentheses into the correct forms.

GIANNI VERSACE

Gianni Versace was born in Reggio Calabria, Italy, in 1946. His mother owned a clothing store. While he _____ (1. grow up), he learned about making clothes. In 1972 he _____ (2. move) to Milan to become a fashion designer, and in 1978 he _____ (3. open) his first store. In the same year, he _____ (4. present) his first collection for women. He _____ (5. already design) a leather collection for a company called Complice, but now he worked for himself.

His designs _____ (6. be) brightly colored and sexy, and he used celebrities like Madonna, Tina Turner, and Bon Jovi as models. In 1984 he _____ (7. bring out) his own fragrance for men, Versace l'Homme. On July 16, 1997, while he _____ (8. walk) outside his apartment in South Beach, Miami, he _____ (9. shoot) dead by a stranger. During his life, his fashion empire _____ (10. become) so successful that it was worth over $800 million.

Pronunciation | numbers

9 ▶2.25 Listen to the numbers. Then listen again and repeat.

May 21ˢᵗ   12/04/09   1920s   2010   4,076   1,300,000 $4,375 $78.32   54½   7¾   6.2%   9.3%

10 **SPEAKING EXCHANGE** Student A: Look at page 138. Student B: Look at page 143. You have some information missing. Ask and answer questions to complete your information.

11 **Pair Work** Write five numbers such as dates, prices, or sizes that are important to you. Tell your partner the numbers. Ask questions to find out why each number is important.

Why did you write 2002?   *I graduated in 2002.*   *What did you study?*   *I studied law.*

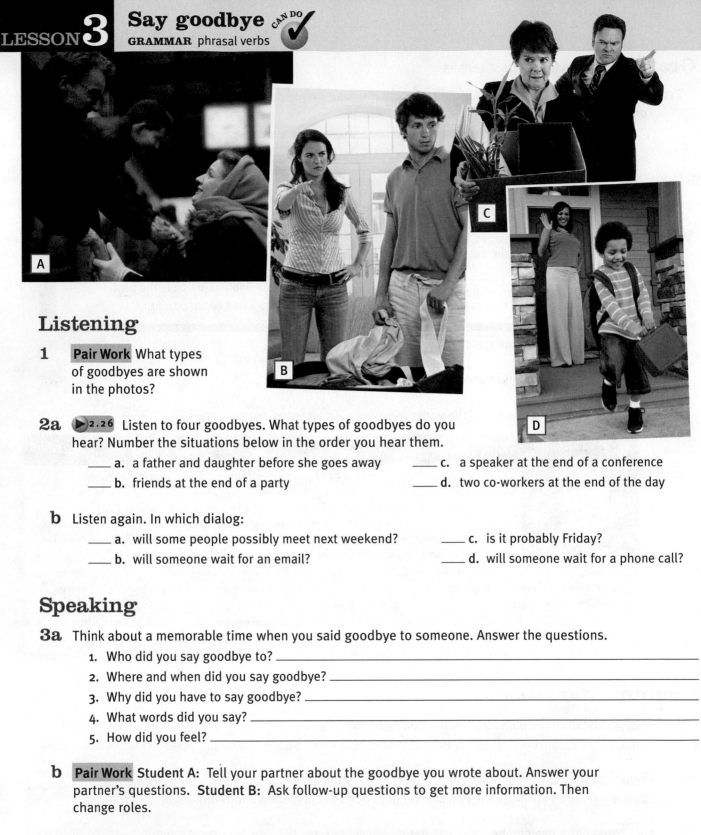

Listening

1 **Pair Work** What types of goodbyes are shown in the photos?

2a ▶2.26 Listen to four goodbyes. What types of goodbyes do you hear? Number the situations below in the order you hear them.

____ **a.** a father and daughter before she goes away   ____ **c.** a speaker at the end of a conference

____ **b.** friends at the end of a party   ____ **d.** two co-workers at the end of the day

b Listen again. In which dialog:

____ **a.** will some people possibly meet next weekend?   ____ **c.** is it probably Friday?

____ **b.** will someone wait for an email?   ____ **d.** will someone wait for a phone call?

Speaking

3a Think about a memorable time when you said goodbye to someone. Answer the questions.

1. Who did you say goodbye to? _____

2. Where and when did you say goodbye? _____

3. Why did you have to say goodbye? _____

4. What words did you say? _____

5. How did you feel? _____

b **Pair Work** **Student A:** Tell your partner about the goodbye you wrote about. Answer your partner's questions. **Student B:** Ask follow-up questions to get more information. Then change roles.

c Read the quotations. What do you think they mean? Do you agree or disagree? Explain your answers.

> "The best things are said last. People will talk for hours saying nothing important and then wait at the door with words that come with a rush from the heart."

> "Don't cry because it's over. Smile because it happened and it was once yours."

Reading

4 **Pair Work** Read about two types of goodbyes. Is there a "good" way to communicate the bad news in these situations?

> **Situation 1: end a relationship**
> You decide that a romantic relationship is not making you happy. You need to tell your boyfriend or girlfriend that you want to break up.

> **Situation 2: fire an employee**
> Your company is doing poorly and must cut its staff. As the officer manager, it is your responsibility to tell five employees that they must leave the company.

5 **SPEAKING EXCHANGE** Student A: Read Part A of the article below. Student B: Read Part B of the article on page 142. Answer the questions.

1. What type of goodbye is described in your article?
2. How did the companies or people say goodbye?
3. What is the conclusion at the end of the article?
4. What do you think of the behavior described in the article?

PART A

How not to fire your staff

One company text-messaged its employees, telling them to call a phone number. A recorded message informed the employees that "All staff who are being retained will be contacted today. If you have not been spoken to, you have lost your job." It's probably not the nicest way to **find out** that you are now unemployed. But it's maybe better than some.

Employees from a technology company **came back** from lunch and found that their security cards didn't work. "What's **going on**?" they asked. The reply? They had been fired.

Another company invited its staff to a conference in Florida. When they **showed up** in the morning, some of the staff were told to go to Room A, others to Room B. The people in Room A listened to a presentation about the company's future. The people in Room B were told they were leaving the company.

It is impossible to **come up with** a "nice" way to fire someone, but managers should at least do it in private and show respect for the employee. The problem is that bosses often panic. They are worried that the fired employees will steal important information. And they are sometimes right: After learning that they were losing their jobs, the staff of one company stole computers and other equipment and nearly destroyed the company's offices.

6 **Pair Work** Explain your part of the article to your partner. Use your answers to Exercise 5 to help you. Then read your partner's article.

7 Look at parts A and B of the article again. Work together to find the phrasal verbs in **bold** that mean the following:

continue	~~canceled~~	arrived	happening	finished a relationship
tolerate	returned	discover	think of/invent	experienced (something bad)

Ex: canceled – *called off*

Grammar | phrasal verbs

8 Which phrasal verbs do the pictures illustrate?

1. _____ 2. _____ 3. _____

9 Look at the Active Grammar box. Then look at the **bold** phrasal verbs in articles A and B in Exercise 5. Decide which type (1–4) each phrasal verb is.

Active Grammar

There are different types of phrasal verbs:

1. The verb takes no object (intransitive).
   *I **showed up** late.*

2. The verb takes an object, and the verb and particle can split* (transitive, separable).
   *I **called off** the wedding.*
   *I **called** the wedding **off**. I **called** it **off**.*

   *When the object is a pronoun (*he/she/it*, etc.), the verb and particle must split.
   NOT: ~~I called off it.~~

3. The verb takes an object, but the verb and particle cannot split (transitive, inseparable).
   *He's **going through** a difficult time.*
   NOT: ~~He's going a difficult time through.~~

4. The verb has a particle and a preposition and doesn't split (transitive, inseparable).
   *We **came up with** a new idea.*
   NOT: ~~We came up a new idea with.~~

See Reference page 136

10 Use words from Box 1 and Box 2 to complete the sentences. Change the verb tenses.

Box 1
go	break	keep
show	put	come
~~call~~		

Box 2
up	on	through
~~off~~	up	up with
back		

Ex: The concert was ___called off___ because the singer was sick.

1. I will not _____ this noise! If it continues, I'll call the police!

2. I don't need a break. I'm going to _____ working.

3. It was a quiet party. There were only six of us, though more people _____ later.

4. She _____ a difficult period when she lost her job, but she's OK now.

5. Couples usually _____ because of jealousy or boredom, or because they find other partners!

6. My best friend is _____ from her vacation tomorrow, so I'm going to the airport to meet her.

Writing

11a Read the thank you letters in the Writing Bank on page 149 and do the exercises.

b Write a thank you letter to a classmate, your teacher, or someone else you know.

Review

1   Complete the sentences using the verbs in parentheses. You may need to add extra words.

   Ex: He has to wash all the dishes. He probably wishes he ___*had*___ (have) a dishwasher.

   1. I have to read so many books! I wish I _____ (be) such a slow reader.
   2. She's so full she can't sleep. She probably wishes she _____ (eat) so much.
   3. I loved Disneyland! I wish I _____ (go) there the last time I was in the US.
   4. He hates taking trains. He wishes he _____ (have) a car.
   5. There are some job openings in the Bahamas. Don't you wish you _____ (can work) there?
   6. My favorite movie was on TV last night, but at 1:00 A.M. I wish they _____ (show) it earlier.

2   Complete the dialogs using the correct forms of the verbs in the box.

   > do   ~~not answer~~   not hear   listen   go   stop   have

   1. A: I knocked on the door last night but you ___*didn't answer*___ (1.). What _____ (2.)?
      B: Oh, sorry. I _____ (3.) to music and I _____ (4.) you.

   2. A: _____ (5.) a good weekend?
      B: Yes, we _____ (6.) on a picnic.
      A: In the rain?
      B: No! The rain _____ (7.) by the time we got to the park.

3   Write sentences using the words in parentheses in the past perfect or past continuous.

   Ex: We tried to call her.
   She/turn off/her cell phone ___*She had turned off her cell phone.*___

   1. I saw a friend after many years. She looked very different.
      She/change/a lot _____
   2. The book was completely new to me.
      I/never/read/before _____
   3. Javed didn't break the window at midnight.
      He/sleep/in his room/at midnight _____
   4. Lola went to an interview every day.
      She/look for/a job _____
   5. I couldn't travel to Mexico for the conference.
      I/lose/my/passport _____

4   Circle the two possible endings for each sentence.

   Ex: They came up with (a great idea)(a solution to the problem)/brilliantly.

   1. We broke up *after many years/because we argued a lot/my husband*.
   2. They showed up *on time/very well/to watch the game*.
   3. We called off *the party/my friends/our engagement*.
   4. I put up with *the excellent service/the noise/those stupid comments*.
   5. He won't find out *if we don't tell him/about the money/of the story*.
   6. What's going on *wrong/here/today*?
   7. I'd like to keep on *working/playing golf/to watch the movie*.

Communication | talk about your memories

5a Spend a few minutes studying the squares in the game below.

b **Group Work** Read the instructions and play The Memory Game.

The Memory Game

How to play

1. Work in groups of three or more. Each player selects a counter, such as a coin, and puts it on START.
2. Roll the die and move the correct number of squares.
3. Talk about the topic in the square.
4. The next student rolls the die, moves, talks, and so on.
5. The first person to reach the FINISH is the winner.

Talk about . . .

START

| happy memories from your childhood | the best movie you have ever seen | your first school | your grandmother or grandfather | a beautiful place you have been to |

the first record or CD you bought and music you used to listen to

an older person you admire

a story or joke you have never forgotten

you ten years ago

an interview you have gone on (job, college, etc.)

the first time you earned some money and what you did with it

FINISH

how your home town has changed in your lifetime

how you met your best friend

a story you have heard in the news recently

something you loved doing as a child

the best present you have ever had

your best birthday

an interesting person you met

a TV show you used to watch as a child

a place you wish was just for you

a place you didn't like in the past

your favorite food and the first things you learned to cook

a favorite book

the house you lived in when you were younger

a wedding you have been to

a restaurant you like going to

a sport or hobby you don't do any more

the most precious thing you own

a special day you remember

a city you know well

Unit 1 Reference

Auxiliary verbs: *do*/*be*/*have*

Use the auxiliary verbs *do*, *be*, and *have* to form tenses and make questions, short answers, and negatives.

Use the verb *do* as the auxiliary verb with the "simple" tenses, except if the main verb is *be*.

> **Does** he smoke? Yes, he **does**. No, he **doesn't**.
> When **do** you have breakfast?
> I **don't** have breakfast.
> **Are** you hungry? NOT: ~~Do you hungry?~~

Use the verb *be* with continuous forms.

> I **am (not)** studying German.
> **Are** you studying? Yes, I **am**. No, I'm not.

Use *have* to make perfect verb forms.

> I **have**/**haven't** finished my book.
> **Have** you finished? Yes, I **have**. No, I **haven't**.

Simple present and present continuous

Use the **simple present** for:

1. habits and routines.
   > Seung-Ah **starts** work at eight o'dock.

2. things that are always true or permanent.
   > Spain **is** a hot country.

3. describing a state or situation.
   > Dimitri **is** really happy about his new job.

Use the **present continuous** for:

1. things that are happening now at this precise moment.
   > Jade **is taking** a shower.

2. temporary situations that are happening around now (but not at this exact moment).
   > I **am learning** Spanish for my job.

Some verbs are used in the simple present and present continuous, but their meaning changes.

> We're **having** a wonderful vacation. (*have* = action/experience—can be used in the continuous)
> We **have** a lovely room by the sea. (*have* = possess—can't be used in the continuous)

The following verbs are not usually used in the continuous form: *like, love, hate, have (possess), need, want, prefer, find, know, realize, believe, understand, remember, seem, suppose, mean, see, hear, smell, taste.*

Present perfect and simple past

Use the **present perfect** to describe:

1. an action that started in the past and continues in the present (unfinished time).
   > I **have known** her since I was a child. (I met her when I was a child and I still know her.)

2. an action that happened in the past but has a result in the present (present result).
   > Tom **has left** his bag at home. (He doesn't have it now.)

Use the **simple past** to talk about something that happened at a specific time (details).

> My mother **called** me yesterday.

for and *since*

The present perfect is often used with *for* and *since*. Use *for* + period of time and *since* + point in time.

> I've known her **for** two months/**since** April.

Phrasal verbs

Form: verb + one or two prepositions (or adverb)

> He **grew up** in France. I **got along with** her.

A phrasal verb can have more than one meaning.

> Take off. The plane **took off** at 6:00. I **took off** my coat.

The meaning often has no connection with the verb.

> We **ran out of** money. (= There is none left.)

Phrasal verbs are often informal or spoken English. Often there is a formal word which means the same.

> The bomb will **go off**. (= The bomb will explode.)

Unit Vocabulary

Relationships

boss	co-worker	teammate
husband	stepmother	acquaintance
stranger	lose touch	father-in-law
classmate	ex-girlfriend	keep in touch
friend of a friend		close/old/best friend
have a lot in common		enjoy his/her company
get along		get to know him/her
have the same sense of humor		

Verbs/adjectives + prepositions

belong to	crazy about	use (something) for
talk about	worry about	spend money on
good at	interested in	

Unit 2 Reference

The passive voice

Form: the verb *be* + past participle

Antonio **is paid** a lot of money.

Are you **being followed**?

We **were given** a new car to drive.

She **has been told** this before.

In **active sentences**, the person (or thing) who does the action comes first.

The man **kissed** the baby.

In **passive sentences**, the person (or thing) affected by the action comes first and is the main focus.

The baby **was kissed** by the man.

The person (or thing) who did the action is often not known or not important.

The movie **has been shown** since 1959. (It isn't important who has shown it.)

Use *by* to include the person (or thing) who did the action in a passive sentence.

The book **was written by** Gong Ji-young.

The passive often sounds impersonal. It is used in formal English and often in the news.

The President **was asked** to resign. (It isn't important who asked him to resign.)

Relative clauses

A clause is part of a sentence. A **defining relative clause** makes it clear who or what you are talking about in a sentence. It gives essential information.

The man **who lives next door** had an accident.

Relative clauses begin with relative pronouns:

who for people	*where* for locations
when for time	*whose* for possessions
which for things or animals	

Don't use *what* as a relative pronoun.

The vase **that** I broke was very expensive.

NOT: ~~The vase what I broke was very expensive.~~

Informal English often uses *that* instead of *who* or *which*.

The police caught the man **that** robbed the bank.

When the verb after the relative pronoun has a different subject, *who* and *which* can be omitted.

The movie which I saw was called Caterpillar. (The subject of *saw* is "*I*" not "*the movie.*")

The movie I saw was called Caterpillar.

The boy who she met was nice. (The subject of *met* is "*she*" not "*the boy.*")

The boy she met was nice.

Simple past and past continuous

The past continuous form: *was/were +___ing*

Use the **past continuous** to talk about what was happening at a particular moment in the past.

What **were** you **doing** at 10 o'clock last night?

It is often used at the beginning of stories to explain the situation.

This happened several years ago. I **was staying** by the sea with friends. We **were having** lunch on the beach . . .

Use the **simple past** for complete, finished actions in the past.

When the simple past and past continuous are used together, the past continuous refers to the longer, background action or situation. The simple past refers to the shorter action or main event that happened to interrupt it.

I **was walking** through the park when the storm **began**.

Use the **past continuous** for temporary actions and situations.

I **was living** in São Paulo last summer.

Use the **simple past** for longer or permanent situations.

I **lived** in Los Angeles for ten years when I was a child.

Unit 3 Reference

Talking about the future

Use **be going to** to talk about plans for the future or intentions (things you have already decided to do).

> *I am going to take a vacation in March.*
> *Sue isn't going to buy that car.*

Use the **present continuous** to talk about fixed future arrangements (usually involving another person). The verbs *go* and *come* often use the present continuous.

> *I am meeting Sam at 2 P.M.* (I called him this morning to arrange it.)
> *Are you coming to the movie tonight?* (You have been invited.)

In many cases, either *be going to* or the present continuous are used.

> *I am playing rugby tomorrow.*
> *I am going to play volleyball.*

Use **will/won't** for unplanned decisions (made while speaking), offers, or promises.

> *Will you carry this box for me?*
> *I won't tell her I saw you.*

For general predictions, use *will* or *be going to*.

> *I think Brazil will win/is going to win the next World Cup.*

Future possibility

Use *will/won't* + adverb to say how likely something is in the future. *Will* comes before the adverb. *Won't* comes after the adverb in negative sentences.

> *I will definitely go.* (you are certain)
> *I certainly won't go.* (you are certain)
> *I will probably stay.* (very certain)
> *I probably won't stay.* (very certain)

Use *may/might/could* when not certain. Do not use *could* in the negative.

> *Alice may meet us later for dinner.*
> *The store might not be open.*

With modal verbs (*will, may, might, could*), use the base form of the verb.

Comparatives and superlatives

One-syllable adjectives, or two-syllable adjectives ending in -y

Adjective	Comparative	Superlative	Notes
old	*older*	*oldest*	Add -er, -est
big	*bigger*	*biggest*	Double the consonant and add -er, -est.
large	*larger*	*largest*	Ends in -e, just add -r, -st
friendly	*friendlier*	*friendliest*	Ends in -y, change -y to -i and add -er, -est

Two (or more)-syllable adjectives

Adjective	Comparative	Superlative	Notes
useful	*more/less useful (than)*	*(the) most/ least useful*	Add *more* (+), or *less* (–), (the) most (++), or (the) least (– –)

Irregular adjectives

> *good/better (than)/(the) best   bad/worse (than)/(the) worst*
> *far/further (than)/(the) furthest or (far/farther/farthest)*

(not) as + adjective + as
If two things are the same, use *as* + adjective + *as*. For negative comparisons, use *not as* + adjective + *as*.

> *The train is as expensive as flying.   It's not as warm as last week.*

Unit Vocabulary

Home

attic	house	balcony	apartment	yard
deck	duplex	elevator	townhouse	pool
stairs	garden	fireplace	basement	
porch	garage	(2) stories	hardwood/carpeted floors	

Adjectives describing places

ugly	noisy	spacious	cramped	old-fashioned
dark	sunny	touristy	unspoiled	picturesque
tiny	clean	modern	polluted	enormous
dull	lively	peaceful	historical	dirty

Compound nouns

DVD player	alarm clock	air conditioner
cell phone	burglar alarm	washing machine

Unit 4 Reference

Factual conditional with *if/ when/unless/as soon as*

To talk about real possibilities in the future, use *if* + **simple present** + *will/can/should/may* (and other modal verbs). *If* + *will* is not usually used in conditional sentences.

> *If* it **rains**, I **will stay** at home.
>
> *If* he **stays** here, he **should learn** the language.
>
> *If* it **rains** I **won't go** out. *If* it **doesn't rain**, I **will go** out.

Unless means *if not*.

> *Unless* it rains, I will go out. *(If it doesn't . . .)*

Use *when* to show the situation is 100% certain.

> **When I wake up tomorrow**, I will make breakfast. (It is certain that I will wake up tomorrow.)

Use *as soon as* to emphasize that an event happens immediately.

> I'll tell him **as soon as** I see him.

Use *If* + **simple present** + **simple present** to talk about things that are always true.

> *If* I **have** time, I **go** to the gym. *(a fact)*
>
> *If* you **don't drink** for a month, you **die**. (scientific fact)

Modals of obligation and prohibition

Obligation

Have to is often used for rules and regulations.

> You **have to show** your passport at Customs.

Must is often used when the obligation comes from the speaker. *Must* is never followed by *to*.

> I **must stop** smoking.

Prohibition

Must not/can't means it is not allowed.

> You **must not/can't leave** your luggage unattended.

No obligation

Don't have to means there is a choice.

> You **don't have to wear** a suit to work.

Recommendation

> You **should** go.
>
> We **shouldn't** stay late.

Question tags

Use question tags in spoken English to check information and to keep the conversation going.

To make question tags, repeat the auxiliary verb, not the main verb. If the main verb is *be*, repeat that.

Affirmative statements use a negative tag. Use this structure when you think the answer is *yes*.

> It**'s** cold in here, **isn't** it?
>
> They **are** French, **aren't** they?
>
> We **have** been there, **haven't** we?

Negative statements use a positive tag. Use this structure when you think the answer is *no*.

> We **don't** have to pay, **do** we?
>
> I **won't** be needed, **will** I?

If there is no auxiliary verb, use *do*, *does*, *did*, or their negatives.

> She **went** home, **didn't** she?
>
> I **know** you, **don't** I?

Short answers also use the auxiliary verb.

> A: She doesn't eat meat, does she?
>
> B: No, she **doesn't**.
>
> A: We have finished the bread, haven't we?
>
> B: Yes, we **have**.

Unit Vocabulary

Time and money

have (money) to spare	a good value
use your (time) wisely	a waste of money
worth spending money on	

Phrasal verbs

pick up	grow up	drop out of
end up	figure out	catch up with
make up	run out of	break up with

Personal qualities

cheap	ambitious	good with numbers
tolerant	generous	good with people
confident	extravagant	work long hours

Unit 5 Reference

Present perfect and present perfect continuous

Use the **present perfect continuous** to talk about:

1. unfinished actions which started in the past and continue in the present. The present perfect continuous emphasizes the continuation of the activity.

   I've been reading your novel. (I haven't finished.)

   BUT *I've read your novel.* (I've finished it.)

2. recently finished activities with present results that often can be seen.

   A: *Why are you hot?*

   B: *I've been running.* NOT: ~~I've run.~~

3. situations that focus on the activity and not the result.

   I've been studying. (This is why I haven't seen you.)

   BUT *I've finished my work.* (Now I can see you.)

How long is often used to focus on the activity. *How much/many* is often used to focus on the result.

   How long have you been saving money? (I want to know about the activity.)

   How much money have you saved? (I want to know about the result.)

Don't use the present perfect continuous with stative verbs: *know, be, like,* etc.

Verb patterns with *-ing* or infinitive

1. Verbs followed by *-ing* (gerund):

   can't stand, enjoy, don't mind, avoid, dislike, adore

2. Verbs followed by the infinitive:

   agree, promise, want, choose, decide, forget, refuse, expect

3. Many verbs can use the pattern: verb + somebody + infinitive:

   allow, help, want, remind, advise, invite, tell

4. Some verbs can be followed by both forms:

   begin, start, continue, stop, remember, like, love, hate, prefer

Sometimes the meaning changes.

I stopped smoking. = I gave up the habit.

I stopped to smoke. = I had a cigarette.

Count and non-count nouns

Count

A count noun can be singular or plural. Countable nouns can be counted. With singular count nouns use *a* or *an*.

   *She eats **an apple** a day. I love eating **apples**.*

Non-count

Non-count nouns have only one form, no singular or plural. Non-count nouns cannot be counted.

   ***some** rice/**a kilo of** rice* NOT: ~~one rice, two rices~~

   *In Asia people eat **rice** with every meal.*

A rice is incorrect, so specify *a . . . of . . .*

   ***A cup of** coffee, **a bottle of** water. . .*

Non-count nouns are generally not used in the plural, for example, *information, news, hair, advice, paper.*

   *Can I have **some information**?* NOT: ~~informations~~

Some non-count nouns are used only in plural form, for example, *scissors, jeans*

   *I bought **some jeans**/**a pair of jeans**.* NOT: ~~a jeans~~

Quantifiers

Count	Non-count
some/(not) any	*some/(not) any*
many	*much*
a few/a couple of	*a little*
a lot of	*a lot of*

Unit Vocabulary

Spare time activities

yoga	fishing	aerobics
chess	jogging	swimming
cards	puzzles	computer games
reading	painting	volleyball
guitar	cooking	exercise
skiing	bicycling	martial arts
soccer	dancing	

Describing movies and books

plot	soundtrack	main character
stars	description	was written by
is set in	is about	was directed by

Unit 6 Reference

Past perfect

Past perfect form: *had/hadn't* + past participle

Use the **simple past** to talk about something that happened in the past. *I **was** ill.*

Use the **past perfect** to talk about what happened before that. *I **had eaten** something bad.*

Use it to make the order of events clear.

*I **was** ill because **I'd eaten** something bad.*

```
        I had eaten
        something bad    I was ill    now
    ────────X───────────────X──────────X──────▶
```

*I **went** to Bali last year. I **hadn't been** there before.*

Do not use the past perfect when the sequence of events in the past is clear.

*I **came** home and **turned** on my computer.*

The past perfect uses many of the same expressions as the present perfect (*since, for, already*).

*I **had worked** there **since** 1993.*

*She **had been** my teacher **for** eight years.*

*I **had already studied** Spanish before I started my Italian course.*

By the time + simple past + past perfect is often used.

***By the time** I **arrived** the party **had finished**.*

Uses of *like*

Use *like* to talk about:

1. personal preferences.
   *I **like** fresh coffee. Harry **doesn't like** swimming.*

2. a specific preference for the future.
   *I **would like** a window seat, please.*

3. general descriptions.
   *What is your new school **like**?*
   *I have never been to Paris. What's it **like**?*

4. things being similar to other things or acting in a similar way to other things.
   *It smells **like** chocolate. He eats **like** a horse.*

5. physical appearance.
   *What does he **look like**?*
   *Sam **looks like** a movie star.*

   Looks like also means *seems like*.
   *It **looks like** Rachel is going to be late again!*

Articles

a/an

Use *a/an*:

1. when it's the first time the subject is mentioned.
   *Last night I saw **a** ghost!*

2. with jobs. *She's **a** doctor, he's **an** engineer.*

the

Use *the*:

1. when it is already known which one is being talked about (it has been mentioned previously).
   *What did **the** ghost look like?*

2. when the subject is unique (there's only one).
   *He's **the** president of the United States.*

3. with superlatives.
   *It's **the** best movie.*

No article

Use no article to make generalizations:

1. with plural nouns. ***Pants** are warmer than **skirts**.*

2. with uncountable nouns. ***Progress** is possible.*

Articles in place names

Use no article:

1. with most place names. *Busan, Korea*

2. with names with South, East, etc. *South America*

Use *the*:

1. for countries with the word *State, Kingdom,* or *Republic*.
   ***the** United States, **the** United Kingdom*

2. for plural names. ***the** Philippines*

3. for rivers, seas, oceans, or deserts. ***the** Seine River*

4. for describing where in a country. ***the** south of France*

Unit Vocabulary

Types of vacations

skiing	camping	beach
safari	sightseeing	amusement park
cruise	adventure	spa resort

Words to describe vacations

romantic	expensive	interesting
convenient	exciting	unforgettable
dangerous	relaxing	peaceful

Unit 7 Reference

Subject and object questions

Object questions

When a *Wh-* question word is the object of the question, use the normal question word order. Most questions are object questions.

Form: Question word + auxiliary + subject + verb

__Who did__ you __shout__ at?

__What did__ you __buy__?

Subject questions

When a *Wh-* question word is the subject of the question, the word order is the same as an affirmative sentence (there is no inversion and no use of an auxiliary verb).

Form: Subject + verb + object

__Who yelled__ at you? NOT: ~~Who did yell at you?~~

__What happened__? NOT: ~~What did happen?~~

used to and *would*

I __used to live__ in Tokyo.

She __didn't use to like__ olives.

__Did__ you __use to live__ in Mexico? Yes, I did./No, I didn't.

She __wouldn't return__ my phone calls.

__Would__ your parents __yell__ at you for being late?

There is no *d* in the spelling of *use to* in negatives and questions.

We __didn't use to__ like our teacher.

__Did__ you __use to__ study art?

Use *used to* to talk about past habits and states which are no longer true. Use *would* to talk about past habits only.

They __used to/would meet__ every day. (past habit)

I __used to love__ him. NOT: ~~I would love him.~~ (past state)

Use the simple past, not *used to*, to describe how long something lasted.

I __worked__ in Italy for five years.

NOT: ~~I used to work in Italy for five years.~~

Use the simple past, not *used to/would*, to talk about a single event in the past.

I __broke__ my leg skiing.

NOT: ~~I used to break my leg skiing.~~

Modals of ability, past and present

Use *can* + verb to describe general ability in the present.

I __can swim__ but I __can't dive__.

Use *could* + verb to describe general ability in the past.

I __could speak__ Spanish, but I __couldn't speak__ Chinese when I was at school.

Use *was able to* to talk about general ability in the past or a particular situation in the past.

I __was able to swim__ twenty miles when I was younger.

I __was able to save__ up for the car that I wanted.

To emphasize that the action is difficult, use *manage to* in the present or past.

I usually __manage to visit__ forty countries every year.

I __managed to finish__ the book but it was very boring.

In the negative, use *couldn't, wasn't able to,* and *didn't manage to* for one particular moment.

I __couldn't buy__ the tickets.

I __wasn't able to buy__ the tickets.

I __didn't manage to buy__ the tickets.

Unit Vocabulary

Education

a fast learner	a strict teacher
learn by heart	a steep learning curve
learn by doing	pick (something) up

practice makes perfect

take a class/a test/lessons/notes

do an exercise/homework/research/an assignment

get a degree/a failing grade/a passing grade/ a report card/homework/a tutor

Describing teachers

1. **adjectives**

patient	understanding	knowledgeable
boring	frightening	
inspiring	open-minded	

2. **verbs**

lose one's temper   talk slowly

ask difficult questions

give clear answers to your questions

punish students who behave badly

Aging

retire	nursing home	senior citizen
elderly	personal philosophy	

Unit 8 Reference

Unreal Conditional

To talk about an unreal, imaginary, or hypothetical situation and its consequences, use: **If + simple past + would('d)/wouldn't.**

> **If I had** a car, **I would** drive to work.
>
> **I'd** live in Jamaica **if I could live** anywhere.

The *if* clause can come first or second in the sentence. If it is first, there is a comma before the result clause.

Use *would*, *could*, or *might* in the result clause.

> If he had a change of heart, I **might forgive** him.

When the subject is *I* and the verb is *be*, say *If I was* or *If I were*.

> **If I were** you, I wouldn't wear that dress again!

Use the real conditional to talk about possible or real situations (*if* + simple present + *will('ll)/won't*).

> **If I go** to France, **I will visit** the Louvre.

Adverbs

An adverb is usually made by adding *-ly* to the adjective.

> *interesting—interesting***ly**   *quick—quick***ly**

Some adverbs are irregular.

> *good (adj)—***well** *(adv)*   *hard (adj)—***hard** *(adv)*
>
> *Do you feel* **well**?   *Natasha works* **hard**.

Some adjectives look like adverbs because they end in *-ly*, but they are not. (For example: *silly, lovely, lively.*)

1. **Adverbs of manner** describe how something happens—they modify the verb. They usually come after the verb.

   > *The news* **spread quickly** *around the office.*
   > *He* **held** *the baby* **gently**.

2. **Adverbs of frequency/probability** describe how often something happens or how probable it is. They usually come before the main verb.

   > *Newspapers* **rarely report** *on these important issues.*
   > *We could* **possibly catch** *the last train.*

3. **Adverbs of degree** modify an adjective or a verb. They make it weaker or stronger.

   > *It was* **totally unexpected**. *He's* **really late**.
   > *She* **absolutely loves** *her job.*

4. Adverbs may also be used as **discourse markers** which describe the speaker's attitude towards the information in the clause.

   > **Luckily**, *the money was still there when I returned.*
   > **Sadly**, *we missed the end of the movie.*

Past unreal conditional

Use this form to talk hypothetically about past situations and to imagine different consequences.

If clause: *If* + subject + past perfect

Main clause: subject + *would have* + past participle

> **If there hadn't been** so much traffic on the highway, I **would have gotten** to the meeting on time.

To indicate possibility, rather than certainty, use *might have/could have* instead of *would have*.

> **If she had studied** harder, she **might have passed** her test.

These unreal past situations have unreal past results.

> **If I had studied** art, I **would have been** happier.
> **If she hadn't left** work early, she **might have finished** the report.
> **Would** you **have been** happier **if you had stayed** at home?

Sometimes the unreal past situation has a present result. (*If* + past perfect + *would* + verb)

> **If I had finished** my university degree, I **would be** an architect now.

Unit Vocabulary

Expressions about change
it's time for a change
that's a nice change
have a change of heart
(do something) for a change

Global issues

security/crime	lifestyle/standard of living
disease/cure	famine/starvation
problems/solutions	the environment/pollution
developed countries/developing countries	

Life decisions

leave a job	start a business
change careers	go to college
buy a home	leave your country
have a baby	start/give up a hobby
retire	

Unit 9 Reference

Reported speech: statements

When reporting what someone said, the verbs often shift into the past because what the person said is in the past.

Will → would

"*I'll go tomorrow.*" *He said he **would** go the next day.*

Simple present tense → simple past tense

"*I **live** in São Paolo.*" *She said she **lived** in São Paolo.*

Present continuous → past continuous

"*I'**m working** for a fashion company.*"
*He said he **was working** for a fashion company.*

Present perfect/simple past tense → past perfect

"*I'**ve been** here for three months.*"
*She told me she **had been** there for three months.*

Time references can also change in reported speech.

"*Call me later **today** or **tomorrow**.*"
*She told me to call her later **that day** or **the next day**.*

Pronouns also change in reported speech.

"*I'll see **you** soon.*" *He said **he** would see **us** soon.*

If what the person said is still true, keep the present tense.

"*I still **love** you.*" *He said he still **loves** me.*

Look at the verb patterns for *say/tell/ask. Say* cannot be followed by a person. *Tell* must be followed by a person.

*She **said** (that) it was late.* NOT: ~~She said me~~ . . .
*He **told me** that I was special.* NOT: ~~He told that~~ . . .
*He **told me** to lock the door.* NOT: ~~He told to me~~ . . .

Reported speech: questions

In reported questions, the word order is the same as in affirmative statements.

"*What time **is it**?*" *He asked me what time **it was**.*

The auxiliary verb (*do/does/did*) is not used.

"*What **do you want**?*" *He asked me what I wanted.*

NOT: ~~He asked me what did I want.~~

In *Yes/No* questions, *ask* is followed by *if/whether.*

*She **asked** me **if/whether** I knew the way.*

make/let/allow

Use *make* + object + verb (without *to*) to talk about obligation imposed by another person or set of rules.

*My father **makes me clean** my room.*
*She **didn't make/never made us** work very hard.*

Use *let* + object + verb (without *to*) to talk about permission. It is not possible to use *let* in the passive form.

*My mom **lets/doesn't let me drive**.*

Use *allow* + object + *to* + verb to talk about permission. The meaning is similar to *let.*

*My parents **allow me to stay** out late.*

Passive form: *be allowed to* + verb.

*They **weren't allowed to borrow** the money.*

Past obligation/permission

To talk about obligation in the past, use ***had to*** + verb.

*We **had to dress** professionally, but we **didn't have to wear** suits.*

To talk about permission in the past, use ***allow*** (see above) and ***could*** + verb.

*We **could watch** TV but we **couldn't stay** up late.*

Unit Vocabulary

Work

promoted	self-employed	dress code
overtime	flexible hours	raise

-ed/-ing adjectives

tired/-ing	frightened/-ing	exhausted/-ing
excited/-ing	confused/-ing	relaxed/-ing
bored/-ing	depressed/-ing	

Job skills and responsibilities

organizing	solving problems
delegating	persuading people
prioritizing	making decisions
dealing with people	working under pressure
working accurately	working irregular hours

Unit 10 Reference

I wish/if only

Use *wish* to express wanting something to be different from reality.

To talk about a wish in the present or a permanent wish, use **wish + simple past**. The most common verbs are *wish + were* and *wish + had*.

> She **wishes** she **were** taller.
>
> I **wish** I **had** a pen.

To talk about a wish in the past, use **wish + had + past participle**.

> He **wishes** he **had gone** to the play yesterday.
>
> I **wish** I **hadn't eaten** that sandwich.

Use **wish + object + would** to show you want something to change. This structure is often used to show anger or annoyance.

> I **wish** she **would come** on time.
>
> I **wish** you **wouldn't make** that noise.

Use **wish + could** to talk about an ability that you want but don't have. *Wish + couldn't* aren't usually used.

> I **wish** I **could play** chess as well as you.
>
> I **wish** I **could fly**.

If only can be used instead of *I wish*. The meaning is a little bit stronger than *I wish*.

> **If only** we could go home! (I wish we could.)
>
> **If only** they hadn't taken the money! (I wish they hadn't.)

Review of past tenses

The simple past, past perfect, and past continuous are often used for narratives.

The simple past is used for the main completed events.

> I **took** the money and **ran**.

The past perfect is used for an action that happened before another action.

> I **hadn't planned** to walk, but **I'd left** my wallet at home.

The past continuous is used for an action in progress over a period of time. It's often a background action in the narrative.

> When I got outside, it **was raining** hard.
>
> I **was living** in Paris when I married Lily. I had met her in Austria.

Phrasal verbs

There are four main types of phrasal verbs.

1. intransitive

The verb has no object.

> I **grew up**.

2. transitive—separable

The verb has an object, and the verb and particle can split.

> I **turned off** the light.
>
> I **turned** the light **off**.
>
> I **turned** it **off**.

When the object is a pronoun (*he/she/it,* etc.), the verb and particle must split.

> NOT: I turned off it.

3. transitive—inseparable

The verb can take an object, but the verb and particle cannot split.

> He **got on** the bus./He **got on**.
>
> NOT: He got the bus on.

4. three-part

The verb has a particle and a preposition. The particle cannot split. (transitive, inseparable)

> We're **looking forward to** seeing you.
>
> NOT: We're looking seeing you forward to.

Unit Vocabulary

Memory

lose	forget	remember	remind us of
miss	remind	remind us to	in memory of

Personal qualities

talented	brilliant	be involved in
inspire	encourage	determined
dedicate (one's life)		

Phrasal verbs

go on	find out	come back
call off	break up	come up with
keep on	wake up	go through
show up	put up with	

Speaking Exchange

Unit 2 | Page 25, Exercise 9a

Group A

Complete the quiz questions with the correct relative pronouns.

Category: Sports

1. The soccer player _____ won the World Cup when he was seventeen years old was
   (a) Pelé. (b) Maradona. (c) David Beckham.
   (d) Ronaldo. ($100,000)

2. The boxer _____ went to prison for refusing to fight in the war against Vietnam was
   (a) Joe Frazier. (b) Muhammad Ali. (c) George Foreman. (d) Sugar Ray. ($100,000)

3. The USSR is the only country _____ team has beaten the US in the Olympic Games at
   (a) baseball. (b) basketball. (c) volleyball.
   (d) swimming. ($100,000)
   [Answers: 1. a, 2. b, 3. b]

Category: The Arts

4. A haiku is a type of poem _____ has
   (a) 14 lines. (b) a male hero. (c) 3 lines.
   (d) a description of an animal. ($100,000)

5. Jackson Pollock was one of the artists _____ invented (a) Cubism. (b) Action Painting.
   (c) Surrealism. (d) Impressionism. ($100,000)

6. The place _____ Mozart, Haydn, and Johann Strauss were born is
   (a) Germany. (b) Switzerland. (c) Poland.
   (d) Austria. ($150,000)
   [Answers: 4. c, 5. b, 6. d]

Category: Geography

7. The name of the desert _____ extends across Mongolia and Northern China is
   (a) the Sahara Desert. (b) the Gobi Desert.
   (c) the Kalahari Desert. (d) the Arabian Desert.
   ($100,000)

8. The name of the river _____ flows both north and south of the Equator is
   (a) the Congo. (b) the Nile. (c) the Mississippi.
   (d) the Amazon. ($100,000)

9. The canal _____ joins the Red Sea and the Mediterranean Sea is (a) the Rhine Canal.
   (b) the Panama Canal. (c) the Suez Canal.
   (d) the Egyptian Canal. ($150,000)
   [Answers: 7. b, 8. a, 9. c]

Unit 2 | Page 20, Exercise 1

Answers

The first newspaper, printed in German, appeared in 1605 in the city of Strasbourg. The technology that resulted in the invention of the radio was developed in the 1890s by Nicola Tesla, Guglielmo Marconi, and others. The first working television system was created by John Logie Baird in Hastings, England, in 1923. Charles Ginsburg, a researcher at Ampex Corporation, developed the first videotape recorder (VTR) in 1952. The origins of the Internet can be found in the ARPANET, a network established in October 1969 to connect the University of California in Los Angeles and the Stanford Research Institute.

Unit 2 | Page 30, Exercise 4

Group A

You want to make money for your newspaper. You like celebrities on the front page. You don't like too many disasters or too much international news because you don't think it sells well. Now look at the list of stories in Exercise 5 on page 30.

Unit 5 | Page 58, Exercise 8a

Problems

1. Customers at your hotel have been complaining that the elevators are too slow and too small. The elevators are old with dark wood paneling on the walls. Replacing the elevators would be very expensive and your hotel does not have enough money. Think of a solution.

2. You own a bookstore in the shopping district of a small town. In the past year, the number of customers visiting your store has decreased. Increasingly, people are buying books online or downloading e-books. If this continues, you will have to close your store. Think of a solution to increase the number of customers who visit your store.

The Man Who Never Lost

USA, 1958. The quiz show contestant was sweating. He nervously looked around the studio where he was being filmed. The television cameras focused on his face. He thought hard. Finally he gave the answer to the question, and the crowd cheered. Millions of Americans watching in their homes were happy that their hero, Charles Van Doren, was again the winner of *Twenty-One*. It was only later that the truth came out. The man whose fame meant that he received 500 letters a day, who appeared on the cover of *Time* magazine, and who had won more than $100,000 on the show, was also a cheat. TV quiz shows were very popular in the US in the 1950s. And the idea that one person could keep on winning was especially popular. Audiences began to support this winner, and wanted to see him win every week. The producer of *Twenty-One*, Dan Enright, decided that to keep his show popular, it was necessary to give Van Doren the answers before the show.

Herbie Stempel, the previous champion before Van Doren, was the person who revealed the truth. He told the public that contestants on the program were given the answers and also taught what to do in front of the cameras: how to look nervous, how to pause, and how to pretend not to know the answers. After an investigation which examined every moment of every *Twenty-One* show, Van Doren eventually admitted cheating. American TV had lost its innocence.

The Stone Angels

Madison Hall. Date: _____

Used Car _____

In good condition, low miles. $ _____

Economic report:

• We made a _____% profit during the fiscal year of 2004, making that year the most successful in the company's long history.

SERVICE STATION

___ MILES

You can save up to **$1,999** on household furnishings if you buy our **Premium package.**

From London Terminals
To Chelmsford
Ticket type Off-peak round-trip

valid on 05/11/03 only

Three-quarters of all accidents take place in the home.
BE CAREFUL!

Unit 6 | Page 71, Exercise 3

Student B

Situation 1: You are in a train station. You would like three round-trip tickets to Boston (two adults and one child). Find out:

1. how much they cost.
2. what time the next train leaves.
3. which track to go to.

Student B

Situation 2: You work in a tourist office. Give directions to the Tate Modern museum.

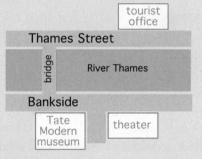

Opening times:
Monday – Thursday: 9:00 A.M. – 5:00 P.M.
Friday/Saturday: 9:00 A.M. – 10:00 P.M.
Closed Sundays

Tickets: adults – £12, children – free

Unit 7 | Page 82, Exercise 8b

Quiz answers

Quiz A

1. Who painted *Guernica* in 1937? Pablo Picasso

2. When did Mozart start composing music? When he was 4 years old/1760

3. Who discovered penicillin in 1928? Sir Alexander Fleming

4. Which of the world's greatest scientists lived from 1879–1955? Albert Einstein

5. Which famous city is nicknamed The Big Apple? New York

6. What invention is Guglielmo Marconi credited with? The radio

Unit 4 | Page 50, Exercise 2b

Student B

How supermarkets persuade you to spend more

How many times has this happened to you? You plan a quick trip to the supermarket to get a few things for supper and, forty-five minutes later, you exit the store with three bags of groceries and an empty wallet.

Supermarkets have always been good at understanding how customers think and using this insight to sell more products. In fact, the shopping cart was invented in the 1940s by a grocer who was looking for a way to increase his sales. He noticed that his customers' purchases were limited by what they could carry. With the new cart, customers could carry more items to their cars. Shoppers appreciated the convenience, thinking "If I buy a lot now, I won't have to come back later." And sales increased.

Another way that supermarkets persuade us to buy more is by creating a pleasant environment. Stores play music to help us relax. Delicious smells from the bakery and deli departments are circulated throughout the store, making our mouths water. These techniques make us want to stay in the store longer. And the longer we stay in the store, the more we buy.

Supermarket tricks:

- Product placement: Supermarkets put the highest profit items at eye level, where they are easiest to see and reach. Often, however, the best bargains are found on the higher or lower shelves.

- Customer loyalty cards: Customers with these cards get lower prices and special discounts, such as "buy one, get one free" deals. However, supermarkets use these cards to gather information about us: what we buy, how often we shop. And they use this information to target us with ads that reflect our shopping habits.

Unit 2 | Page 30, Exercise 4

Group B

You are responsible editors. You want a lot of news about developing countries. You think that major disasters and international news stories are very important. Now look at the list of stories in Exercise 5 on page 30.

Unit 2 | Page 25, Exercise 9a

Group B

Complete the quiz questions with the correct relative pronouns.

Category: Movies

1. Marilyn Monroe was the actress _____ original name was (a) Norma Jean Baker. (b) Mary Monray. (c) Grace Kelly. (d) Jane Monroe Smith. ($100,000)

2. The 1997 movie _____ won 11 Oscars was (a) *The English Patient.* (b) *Star Wars – Episode 1.* (c) *Titanic.* (d) *E.T.: The Extra-Terrestrial.* ($100,000)

3. The man _____ directed *Reservoir Dogs, Pulp Fiction,* and *Kill Bill* is (a) Alfred Hitchcock. (b) Steven Spielberg. (c) Woody Allen. (d) Quentin Tarantino. ($100,000)
[Answers: 1. a, 2. c, 3. d]

Category: Nature

4. The mammal _____ lives the longest is the (a) elephant. (b) turtle. (c) blue whale. (d) lizard. ($100,000)

5. An area of land _____ 2.75m of rain falls every year is (a) New York City. (b) The Alps. (c) The Amazon Rainforest. (d) Europe. ($100,000)

6. The camel is an animal _____ hump is made of (a) water. (b) fat. (c) muscle. (d) hair. ($150,000)
[Answers: 4. c, 5. c, 6. b]

Category: Science and technology

7. The person _____ invented the telephone was (a) John Logie Baird. (b) James Watt. (c) Alexander Watt. (d) Alexander Bell. ($100,000)

8. The small piece of silicon _____ makes a computer work is called a (a) microchip. (b) microphone. (c) microsoft. (d) microscope. ($100,000)

9. Sir Alexander Fleming was the man _____ work in 1941 changed the state of medicine around the world. He discovered (a) AIDS. (b) cancer. (c) penicillin. (d) X-rays. ($150,000)
[Answers: 7. d, 8. a, 9. c]

Unit 6 | Page 76, Exercise 9

Student A

Read these sentences to your partner and continue the conversation. (Make up a response.)

My cousin has twenty brothers!

My best friend has climbed Mount Everest!

My partner works as a spy!

I play six musical instruments!

I learned Chinese, Japanese, and French last year!

I lost my wallet yesterday!

Unit 3 | Page 40, Exercise 9

Student B

CALL YOUR PARTNER.

1. Your partner works in an office (Smith and Co.). Ask to speak to the manager about a job.

2. Your partner works at Capital Bank. Ask to speak to Mr. Jones, the bank manager, about your bank account.

3. Your partner works at the front desk of the Windham Hotel. Ask to speak to Jill Orwell in Room 101.

ANSWER THE PHONE.

1. You work in a computer store (E-Tec Computers). All of the computer service technicians are helping other customers right now.

2. You work in an office (Lula Incorporated). The line is busy.

3. You work in a school (Ace School of English). The director is at lunch until 1:00.

Unit 8 | Page 97, Exercise 11b

1. Asia isn't the biggest continent, but it actually has the most people.
2. Rich countries regularly throw away food, but 50% of the world's people don't have enough to eat.
3. Eighty percent of people in the world don't have electricity or running water.
4. Thirty percent of the world's population can read, and only 1% go to college. Surprisingly, only 1% of the world's population owns a computer.

Unit 2 | Page 30, Exercise 4
Group C

You think that scientific developments are important for the world's future. You also believe that there needs to be a balance between good news and bad news on the front page. Now look at the list of stories in Exercise 5 on page 30.

Unit 4 | Page 50, Exercise 2b
Student C

How salespeople persuade you to spend more

It is said that the best salespeople can sell anything, to anybody, at any time. They do this by using very simple psychological techniques.

Good salespeople understand that people prefer to speak rather than listen. Before talking about their products, skilled salespeople will attempt to understand their customers' needs. By taking the time to ask questions, salespeople build a relationship. If customers think of the salesperson as a friend, they will be more likely to trust his or her advice and become a repeat customer.

Another technique used by salespeople is called mirroring. Research shows that customers feel more comfortable buying from people who are like them. Effective salespeople will try to behave like their customers, copying their personalities and even body language. If a customer makes jokes, the salesperson will, too. If the buyer nods his or her head, the salesperson does also. Salespeople will sometimes repeat the last phrase the customer said, which creates an atmosphere of agreement.

Salesperson tricks:

- Pushy language: Salespeople will choose language that subtly pushes the customer towards buying the product. They will not say "if you buy…" but "when you buy…" so it seems like the decision to buy has already been made.

- "Add-ons": In this technique, salespeople try convince the buyer to purchase additional items associated with a product they have just purchased. For example, a salesperson who has just sold a digital camera will then try to sell the same customer an extended warranty, batteries, memory card, and camera case. Often these additional items earn the store more profit than the original product.

Unit 6 | Page 76, Exercise 9
Student B

Read these sentences to your partner and continue the conversation. (Make up a response.)

My cousin knows Angelina Jolie!

My best friend has been married five times!

My partner is famous!

I eat pasta every single day!

I left home when I was fifteen!

I won the lottery last year!

Unit 7 | Page 82, Exercise 8b
Quiz answers

Quiz B

1. Which islands did Christopher Columbus discover in 1492, before he discovered America? The Bahamas
2. Who painted the Sistine Chapel? Michelangelo
3. Which European country has the smallest area? Vatican City
4. Who wrote the song *Imagine* in 1971? John Lennon
5. What did John Logie Baird invent? The television
6. Which is the world's longest river? The Nile

Unit 10 | Page 116, Exercise 3b
Story endings

1. When Colin left the hospital, his memory began to return. Lydia played him his favorite songs and took him to places they used to go to together. Gradually, he and Lydia fell in love again. They got married and now live happily together.

2. Mr. Nobody's real name is David Rogers. Rogers was a sailor. He was hit on the head during a trip across the Pacific Ocean. At first he seemed OK. But when the ship stopped off in Australia he lost his memory. His real identity was discovered when his family saw a photo of him in the newspaper. Today he doesn't remember all of his past, but he remembers family and friends and everything that happened to him before his last trip by boat.

3. The journalist, S., would imagine himself walking down a street, and in his mind he would see the objects on the street. His incredible memory was the result of what we now call visualization technique. He also had synaesthesia – which means he associated one sense with another. For example, taste can be associated with color. He once said to Luria, "What a crumbly yellow voice you have."

Unit 6 | Page 70, Exercise 8

Choose one of the photos below. Imagine you were one of the people in this situation. Think about what you are going to say, then describe the photo to your partner.

Unit 8 | Page 102, Exercise 6a

Student B

Are you ready FOR CHANGE?

1. Do you always read the same newspaper?	Yes/No
2. Do you like to start new hobbies?	Yes/No
3. Would you like to take a course to learn new skills for work?	Yes/No
4. Do you have many different groups of friends who don't know each other?	Yes/No
5. Do you like to experiment with new recipes when you are cooking?	Yes/No
6. Do you always shop in the same place?	Yes/No
7. (your own question) _____	Yes/No
8. (your own question) _____	Yes/No

Unit 10 | Page 123, Exercise 5

Student B

PART B

How not to break up with your partner

OK, so the rich and famous always say "It was an amicable break-up" or "We **broke up** because of work pressures." Don't believe a word of it. They may **keep on** smiling for the cameras, but behind the smiles there are some angry people. Here are some examples of why.

One famous actress was expecting a baby when her long-term partner, and the father of the child, sent her a fax to inform her that he was leaving her.

But maybe that's not as bad as actor Matt Damon. He split up with girlfriend Minnie Driver on the Oprah Winfrey talk show, live, in front of the US public. Billy Bob Thornton **called off** his relationship with Laura Dern by marrying Angelina Jolie. Dern said, "I left our home to work on a movie and, while I was away, my boyfriend got married and I've never heard from him again."

But if you think they **went through** tough break-ups, times were even harder for women a few centuries ago. Take King Henry VIII's wives. Out of his six wives, he divorced two and he had another two executed. When it's time to say the "Big Goodbye," it seems that women have always had to **put up with** insensitive men.

It's never too late . . .

Juan Lopez, 92, Colombia

At the age of only 19, Juan wrote a short story that was published in a major literary magazine. The year was 1937. It took Juan only 73 years to write his next story. At age 92, Juan published a novel that won several literary awards and appeared on the best-seller list. The title? *Young Love.* "It's kind of like *Romeo and Juliet.*" explains Juan. "A theme of the novel is that, at times, young people have more passion than wisdom. And older people often forget the importance of love."

Why did he wait so long to write the novel? Juan explains that as a younger man he didn't have the life experience or the wisdom to express what he wanted to say. "I just couldn't have written the book even when I was 10 years younger. I knew I had something to say, but I didn't know how to say it. I wasn't ready." Juan believes that he is not unusual—that many elderly people have unique and important stories to tell. "You don't live nine decades without learning something about life. That's special. We have a lot to share with the world."

Jackie Taylor, 83, Australia

Jackie was an avid runner until the age of 79. She has participated in over a hundred marathons in her lifetime. But then she seriously injured her knee at the Sydney Half Marathon. "When I couldn't run anymore, I felt like a part of me had died. I was very depressed."

She couldn't stay inactive, though, and discovered a gentler sport—swimming. "Living so close to the ocean, I tried open-water swimming. What a thrill!" Only after a year of training, Jackie managed to compete in the Cole Classic, Australia's largest ocean swim. For the past three years she has won in the 75+ category. "I know I'm getting older. I respect that, and I accept that my body can't do things it used to. But as long as I can find new ways to exercise, I think I can stay happy."

The Stone Angels

Madison Hall. Date: January 15, 2005

Used Car

In good condition, low miles. $2,500

Economic report:

• We made a 15.6% profit during the fiscal year of _____, making that year the most successful in the company's long history.

SERVICE STATION
1½ MILES

You can save up to $_____ on household furnishings if you buy our **Premium package.**

From London Terminals
To Chelmsford
Ticket type Off-peak round-trip

valid on _____/03 only

_____ of all accidents take place in the home.
BE CAREFUL!

Writing Bank

Unit 1 | Page 13, Exercise 11

Informal emails

1 Read the email and answer the questions.

    1. Why hasn't Mark written recently?

    2. What are Fernando's hobbies?

    3. How does Mark know about Tim's news?

    4. What is Jane studying?

    5. What does Mark invite Fernando to do?

> **Informal greeting**
>
> Hi Fernando,
>
> 1 Thanks for your email. It's great to hear from you. I'm sorry I haven't been in touch for a while, but I've been very busy with work. I've been traveling a lot recently. I've been to Germany, Spain, Brazil, China, and Japan in the last four months!
>
> 2 How are things with you? Are you still doing martial arts and running every day? Have you found a girlfriend yet? Do you remember Tim? I saw him the other day and he's married now and has four children!
>
> 3 Anyway, life here is pretty good. Jane is enjoying her school and is very excited about becoming a teacher. We would love to see you sometime. Why don't you come and visit us next time you are in the US?
>
> 4 Look forward to hearing from you again soon.
>
> All the best,
>
> Mark

Informal language for closing, such as *Best wishes*, *Love*, *All the best*, *Take care*

Writing skill | paragraphs

2 Read the Useful Phrases box. Match these descriptions to paragraphs 1–4 in the email in Exercise 1.

    _____ a. giving your news and making an invitation

    _____ b. introduction and reason for writing or not writing

    _____ c. closing

    _____ d. asking for news/talking about friends.

Useful Phrases

Introduction/reason for (not) writing	*Thanks for your message/email.* *I am writing because . . .* *Sorry I haven't been in touch for a while, but . . .*
Asking for/giving news	*How are (things with) you?/How's it going?* *I hope you are well.* *Please write (back) soon.* *I've been traveling a lot recently.* *I'm attaching/including a photo of . . .*
Closing	*Look forward to hearing from you soon.* *I can't wait to see you.* *Take care.*

Unit 3 | Page 34, Exercise 9a

Formal letter

1 Read the letter and check the correct choice. There may be more than one correct answer.

1. The letter is a
   - ____ a. letter of complaint.
   - ____ b. request for information.
   - ____ c. thank you letter.

2. Mrs. Green would like to
   - ____ a. rent a house near Orlando for two weeks.
   - ____ b. stay in a hotel in Orlando.
   - ____ c. rent a house in Orlando for the month of August.

3. Mrs. Green
   - ____ a. hasn't decided which house she would like to stay in.
   - ____ b. would like a house without a swimming pool.
   - ____ c. wants a house which sleeps up to ten people.

4. Mrs. Green would like to know
   - ____ a. if she can bring her dogs.
   - ____ b. if the houses are safe for children.
   - ____ c. if the company can give her some beds for the children.
   - ____ d. about the other services the company offers.

End with a polite, professional closing, such as *Sincerely, Yours sincerely, Respectfully yours, Kind regards,* or *Yours truly.* If you would like a reply, end the letter with *I look forward to hearing from you.*

Writing skill | paragraphs

2 Read the Useful Phrases box. Match the meanings below to the paragraphs in the letter above.
   - ____ a. general request
   - ____ b. reason for writing
   - ____ c. ask for a reply
   - ____ d. specific details

Use *To Whom It May Concern* if you don't know the name of the person you are writing to. *Use Dear Mr. Black/Mrs. Green* if you know the name. Put a colon (:) after the name.

Write the name or title (example: *Director of Finance*) and address of the person you are writing to.

Sunshine State Properties
255 Orange Ave.
Orlando, FL 32801

332 Dodd St.
Montclair, NJ 07042

Write your address here. Don't write your name.

Write the date here.

May 30, 2012

To Whom It May Concern:

1 I am writing to get some more information about your vacation homes in Florida. According to your website, you have rental homes located near Orlando. I would like to rent a house in that area this summer, and I am therefore interested in getting some more information about a few of the houses.

2 I am looking for a large house with a swimming pool, that will sleep 8–10 people. Ideally, the house would be no more than an hour from Orlando. We would like to rent the house from August 2–15.

3 I would be grateful if you could supply me with the following information:

4 First, I would like to know if either of the houses on Sealark Drive in Lake Butler is available for this period.

5 Second, there are small children in our party. Could you tell me if these two houses are suitable for children? For example, are there fences around the swimming pools? Do the houses have gates for the stairs? In addition, will it be necessary to bring beds for the children, or can you provide these?

6 Finally, could you give me some more details about the services you offer, such as the cleaning service, car rental, etc.?

7 Thank you in advance. I look forward to hearing from you.

Yours sincerely,

Sophie Green

Use formal language. Don't use contractions (*I would like* . . . NOT: ~~I'd like~~).

Useful Phrases

First lines	*I am writing in order to . . .*
	I am writing in response to (your letter) . . .
	I am writing to ask (for information) about . . .
	I am writing to complain about . . .
Last lines	*I would be grateful if you could . . .*
	Could you please send me . . . ?
	I enclose (my résumé/the application form/a check) . . .
	I look forward to hearing from you.
	Thank you in advance.

Writing a summary

1 Read the description of the movie *Babette's Feast* and mark the statements true (*T*) or false (*F*).

_____ 1. The sisters are from Paris.

_____ 2. The sisters are married.

_____ 3. The villagers argue a lot.

_____ 4. Babette works for the sisters.

_____ 5. Babette buys a lottery ticket every year.

_____ 6. Babette saved a lot of money.

_____ 7. Babette decides to leave the village.

_____ 8. The sisters cook a fantastic meal for the village.

_____ 9. The meal is a great success.

_____ 10. After the meal, the villagers continue arguing.

In a tiny village in Jutland, Denmark, two sisters, Phillipa and Martina, live together, caring for their elderly father. A long time ago, the sisters had been famed for their beauty. They both had chances to marry, one to a famous singer, the other to a handsome soldier. Instead, they chose a quiet life beside their father, a life of boiled fish, and the villagers' constant arguing.

Many years later, a woman named Babette arrives from Paris. Her family is dead, and she will now spend her life helping the sisters. For 15 years she serves them for free, working in the house while the sisters look after the very old villagers. Babette's only contact with her former life in France is a lottery ticket that a friend renews every year.

One day, news arrives that Babette has won the lottery. The sisters expect their helper to leave them. But Babette decides to cook a wonderful meal for the village. She imports the finest food from France and begins preparing the meal. At first, the villagers are worried; they know only the simplest of food. But after trying the first courses, the mood changes. The feast—so colorful and delicious-looking that it seems to belong in a dream or a work of art—warms their cold hearts. The villagers stop arguing and remember why they love each other. The movie ends with the villagers holding hands together under a starry sky.

Writing skill | summarizing

2a A summary gives important information in a few words. What type of information is usually cut out from a summary?

b **Pair Work** Read the Useful Phrases box. Then look at the description of *Babette's Feast* again. Decide which information is important to summarize the story and which information you can cut.

Useful Phrases

Contrast	***Instead,*** *they chose a quiet life . . .*
	But *Babette decides to cook a wonderful meal . . .*
Sequence words	***At first,*** *the villagers are worried . . .*
	After *trying the first courses,*
Setting the scene	*In a (tiny village) in (Jutland) . . .*
	Many years later, *a woman named Babette arrives . . .*
Ending	***The movie ends with/In the end,*** *the villagers . . .*

c Rewrite the description of *Babette's Feast*. Summarize the information in 100 words.

Descriptions

1 Read the descriptions of three teachers. Then put the words and phrases in the box into the correct columns below.

> a great imagination   kind and polite
> calm and understanding   knowledgeable
> short, slightly chubby   enthusiastic
> very good-looking   encouraging
> dressed conservatively   a friendly face
> have (her) hair tied back   medium height
> organized, respectful, and interesting

Physical	Clothing	Character
		a great imagination

2 Write any other useful expressions in the columns above.

3 Complete the sentences with words or phrases from the box in Exercise 1.

1. Rosa tells the most amazing stories. She has

   _____.

2. He always wore a dark suit with a tie. He

   _____.

3. She listened carefully to my problems, and was able to help. She was _____

   and _____.

4. He's always eager to start a new job. He's very

   _____.

5. The receptionist smiled, thanked us, and offered to find us a taxi. She was

   very _____ and

   _____.

My favorite teacher was my geography teacher. He was a short, slightly chubby man who was calm and understanding. He would always listen to you, and have some kind words to say, whatever your problem. He was knowledgeable, too, and always explained everything clearly. I will never forget some of the things he taught me.

Mrs. Manley was of medium height and had a very friendly face. She dressed conservatively, but she was very good-looking. She taught history and was very enthusiastic about her subject. She taught it because she loved it, and she made me love it, too. She was always encouraging, and she had a great imagination. The characters and events she described really came to life for me. When she left the school to teach at another school, I missed her very much.

The best teacher I ever had was Miriam Santos. She taught us Latin, and she was organized, respectful, and interesting. She was a tall, skinny lady who wore glasses and always had her hair tied back. She looked fierce, but she was always kind and polite.

4 Think about a teacher from your past and complete the paragraph.

My favorite teacher was my _____

teacher. (S)He was a _____,

_____ (wo)man, who was

_____ and _____.

(S)He would always _____,

and _____. (S)He was

_____ too and always

_____. I will

never forget _____

_____.

147

Newspaper articles

1 Read the article and mark the statements true (*T*), false (*F*), or no information (*NI*).

   ____ **1.** Cigarette smoke is a problem only for smokers.

   ____ **2.** Smoking poisons the air.

   ____ **3.** Second-hand smoke causes lung cancer and heart disease.

   ____ **4.** In New Mexico, 2,100 adults die every year because of second-hand smoking.

   ____ **5.** The Campaign for Tobacco Free Kids was started in 2010.

   ____ **6.** The writer wants new laws to stop people smoking in public.

   ____ **7.** It is difficult to pass laws that protect people from second-hand smoke.

1   Many of us choose not to smoke because of the effects smoking has on the body. But researchers have found that second-hand smoke leads to similar problems.

2   Every time someone lights a cigarette, poisons are released into the air. As a result, everyone inhales the smoke. Studies show that diseases such as lung cancer and heart disease are caused by second-hand smoke.

3   Every year in New Mexico, 2,100 adults die as a result of smoking. Between 230 and 390 of these deaths are caused by second-hand smoking, according to the Campaign for Tobacco Free Kids.

4   Therefore, we need more laws to protect us from second-hand smoke. It's time for a change, and time to make more places safe for our health.

Writing skill | paragraphs

2 Read the Useful Phrases box. Match these descriptions to paragraphs 1–4 in the article in Exercise 1.

   ____ **a.** recommends future action to solve the problem

   ____ **b.** gives statistics to support the argument

   ____ **c.** gives scientific information to support the argument

   ____ **d.** introduces the topic

Useful Phrases

Giving information to support your argument	*Researchers have found that . . .* *Studies show that . . .* *According to scientists . . .*
Giving statistical information	*Every year, 2,100 adults die . . .*
Concluding	*Therefore, we need more laws.* *In conclusion, we need a change.*

Thank you letters

1 Read the letters and answer the questions.

1. Why is Liliana writing?
2. What did they do during Liliana's visit?
3. Why is William Dabbitt writing?
4. Did Ms. Jenkins and her team do a good job? How do we know?

Mygrave-Bapus Financial Consultants
1800 Robson Street
Vancouver, BC
V6G 1C3

Conference coordinator
Cheadle Hotel
1005 Queen St.
Toronto, Ontario
M6J 1J3

July 20, 2012

Dear Ms. Jenkins:

I am writing to thank you for hosting our conference this year. It was a great success. Your efforts were appreciated by all, and several participants commented on the excellent organization. Please also pass on my thanks to your team. I look forward to working with you in the future.

Kind regards,

William Dabbitt

William Dabbitt

November 3, 2012
Bristol

Hi Andrea,

Thanks a lot for letting me stay with you this week. I had a wonderful time. It was great to visit the city and see so many things. I'm sure I'll be back next year. Enjoy the rest of the summer and I hope to see you soon. Keep in touch!

Best wishes,

Liliana

Writing skill | formal/informal

2a Read the Useful Phrases box. Underline examples of these features in the letters. Which letter in Exercise 1 is formal? How do you know?

Useful Phrases

Greeting	**Informal:** *Hi/Hello/Dear Enzo,* **Formal:** *Dear Sir,/Madam, or Dear Mr. Brown,*
Opening line	**Informal:** *Thanks a lot for letting me stay.* **Formal:** *I am writing to thank you . . .*
Comment	**Informal:** *I had a great time.* **Formal:** *Your efforts were appreciated by all.*
Final message	**Informal:** *I hope to see you soon.* **Formal:** *I look forward to working with you . . .*
Goodbye	**Informal:** *Best wishes,/Love,/Lots of love,* **Formal:** *Kind regards,/Yours sincerely,*

b Look at the following features. Are they usually formal (*F*) or informal (*I*)?

_____ 1. full verb forms (We are)   _____ 3. the passive   _____ 5. abbreviations (thanks)

_____ 2. contractions (I'm)   _____ 4. exclamation marks (!)

Pronunciation Bank

Part 1 | ▶ 2.27 English phonemes

Consonants

Symbol	Key word	Symbol	Key word
d	**d**ate	ŋ	goi**ng**
b	**b**ed	s	**s**ofa
t	**t**en	z	**z**ero
p	**p**ark	ʃ	**sh**op
k	**c**ar	ʒ	televi**si**on
g	**g**ame	h	**h**at
tʃ	**ch**ild	m	**m**enu
dʒ	**j**ob	n	**n**ear
f	**f**our	l	**l**ike
v	**v**isit	r	**r**ide
θ	**th**ree	y	**y**oung
ð	**th**is	w	**w**ife

Vowels

Symbol	Key word	Symbol	Key word
i	b**e**	ə	**a**bout
ɪ	s**i**t	eɪ	d**ay**
ɛ	r**e**d	aɪ	b**y**
æ	c**a**t	aʊ	h**ou**se
ɑ	f**a**ther	ɔɪ	b**oy**
oʊ	b**oa**t	ɑr	c**ar**
ɔ	b**ou**ght	ɔr	d**oor**
ʊ	b**oo**k	ʊr	t**our**
u	sh**oe**	ɪr	h**ere**
ʌ	b**u**t	ɛr	th**ere**
ɚ	w**or**d		

Part 2 | ▶ 2.28 Sound-spelling correspondences

Sound	Spelling	Examples
/ɪ/	i	this listen
	y	gym typical
	ui	build guitar
	e	pretty
/i/	ee	green sleep
	ie	niece believe
	ea	read teacher
	e	these complete
	ey	key money
	ei	receipt receive
	i	police
/æ/	a	can man land
/ɑ/	a	pasta
	al	calm
	ea	heart
/ʌ/	u	fun sunny husband
	o	some mother month
	ou	cousin double young
/ɔ/	ou	bought
	au	daughter taught
	al	bald small always
	aw	draw jigsaw
/aɪ/	i	like time island
	y	dry shy cycle
	ie	fries die tie
	igh	light high right
	ei	height
	ey	eyes
	uy	buy
/ɛɪ/	a	lake hate shave
	ai	wait train straight
	ay	play say stay
	ey	they obey
	ei	eight weight
	ea	break
/oʊ/	o	home phone open
	ow	show throw own
	oa	coat road coast
	ol	cold told

Part 3 | ▶ 2.29 Silent consonants

Some letters appear in words where they are not pronounced.

Letter	Silent in:	Letter	Silent in:	Letter	Silent in:
b	dou**b**t clim**b**	h	**h**our w**h**at	p	**p**sychology recei**p**t
c	s**c**issors s**c**ene	k	**k**now **k**nee	s	i**s**land ai**s**le
d	We**d**nesday san**d**wich	l	ta**l**k ca**l**m	t	lis**t**en whis**t**le
g	ou**g**ht lon**g**	n	autum**n** colum**n**	w	**w**rite ans**w**er

Irregular Verbs

Verb	Simple Past	Past Participle	Verb	Simple Past	Past Participle
be	was/were	been	let	let	let
beat	beat	beaten	lie	lay	lain
become	became	become	light	lit	lit
begin	began	begun	lose	lost	lost
bend	bent	bent	make	made	made
bet	bet	bet	mean	meant	meant
bite	bit	bitten	meet	met	met
blow	blew	blown	must	had to	had to
break	broke	broken	pay	paid	paid
bring	brought	brought	put	put	put
build	built	built	read	read	read
burn	burned/burnt	burned/burnt	ride	rode	ridden
burst	burst	burst	ring	rang	rung
buy	bought	bought	rise	rose	risen
can	could	been able	run	ran	run
catch	caught	caught	say	said	said
choose	chose	chosen	see	saw	seen
come	came	come	sell	sold	sold
cost	cost	cost	send	sent	sent
cut	cut	cut	set	set	set
deal	dealt	dealt	shake	shook	shaken
dig	dug	dug	shine	shone	shone
do	did	done	shoot	shot	shot
draw	drew	drawn	show	showed	shown
dream	dreamed/dreamt	dreamed/dreamt	shrink	shrank	shrunk
drink	drank	drunk	shut	shut	shut
drive	drove	driven	sing	sang	sung
eat	ate	eaten	sink	sank	sunk
fall	fell	fallen	sit	sat	sat
feed	fed	fed	sleep	slept	slept
feel	felt	felt	slide	slid	slid
fight	fought	fought	smell	smelled	smelled
find	found	found	speak	spoke	spoken
fly	flew	flown	spell	spelled	spelled
forget	forgot	forgotten	spend	spent	spent
forgive	forgave	forgiven	spill	spilled	spilled
freeze	froze	frozen	split	split	split
get	got	got	spoil	spoiled	spoiled
give	gave	given	spread	spread	spread
go	went	gone/been	stand	stood	stood
grow	grew	grown	steal	stole	stolen
hang	hung	hanged/hung	stick	stuck	stuck
have	had	had	swear	swore	sworn
hear	heard	heard	swell	swelled	swollen/swelled
hide	hid	hidden	swim	swam	swum
hit	hit	hit	take	took	taken
hold	held	held	teach	taught	taught
hurt	hurt	hurt	tear	tore	torn
keep	kept	kept	tell	told	told
kneel	knelt	knelt	think	thought	thought
know	knew	known	throw	threw	thrown
lay	laid	laid	understand	understood	understood
lead	led	led	wake	woke	woken
learn	learned	learned	wear	wore	worn
leave	left	left	win	won	won
lend	lent	lent	write	wrote	written

Audioscript

▶ 1.02 (Page 8)

Dialog 1
A: What clubs do you belong to?
B: I don't belong to any, but my daughter is a member of a chess club.
A: Oh yeah? Is she a good chess player?
B: Yes, she is. She's very good, actually.
A: Does she play a lot?
B: Every day. She always beats me!

Dialog 2
A: What types of exercise do you do?
B: I'm crazy about running.
A: Do you do it regularly?
B: At least three or four times a week.
A: Where do you run?
B: In the park.

Dialog 3
A: Apart from your own, are there any other cultures that you're interested in?
B: I'm really interested in Mexican culture.
A: Have you ever traveled to Mexico?
B: Yes, I have. I went there on vacation a few years ago and just found it fascinating.
A: Really?
B: Yeah, I mean, there are areas that are full of old ruins—at Tulum, for example, there is this walled city on a cliff above the ocean. It's just amazing. Since then I've read a lot of books about Maya and Aztec culture.
A: Are you planning a return trip?
B: Yes, I am. Definitely.

▶ 1.03 (Page 11)

Speaker 1
I met my best friend when I was in college. He lived in the room next door and always played strange, very loud music. I was majoring in Chinese, which was really difficult, and I remember thinking, "He's having a much better time than me!" So one day I just went over and said hello. I got in the habit of going to his room whenever I needed a break from studying. When we graduated college we lost touch for a while, but when we met again we had so much to talk about.

Speaker 2
We actually met when I bumped into Anton's car when I was trying to park. Luckily, there wasn't much damage—just some scrapes on the bumpers. I thought he was going to be angry, but he was very nice about it. Actually, we have the same sense of humor and we both just started laughing. We exchanged phone numbers and then he asked me to have coffee with him. We got to know each other and soon we became really good friends.

Speaker 3
I met Juliet while I was working. I was delivering a package to an office downtown and she was the receptionist. Juliet had a really big smile, and I thought "She looks friendly," so I invited her to a party. We've been friends ever since, and I really enjoy her company. We still go to parties together!

Speaker 4
I've just met a new friend, Bulent, on the Internet. My job is really boring, so I spend a lot of time on the Internet, in chat rooms. Bulent is Turkish, like me, and we've found that we have a lot in common.

Speaker 5
It was a strange place to meet. We were both flying to Moscow, and the plane was delayed for 4 hours! We met in the coffee lounge at the airport, and we started talking. We found out we were flying to the same city and staying in the same hotel! After that trip, we just kept in touch.

▶ 1.04 (Page 14)

Speaker 1
I'd like to talk about Romina. She was my best friend for about 12 years. Before meeting her, most of my friends were boys and I didn't have many girlfriends. We met in college and began studying together and hanging out at night. We developed this method of studying before exams—basically spending the whole night drinking coffee and quizzing each other. It was terrible for our health but good for our friendship. Unfortunately, we're not in touch anymore. We had an argument over money while we were on vacation last year, and we haven't seen each other since then. I miss her.

Speaker 2
My father has been a big influence on me. I really respect him. Um . . . partly because of what he does—he's a doctor—but I think also because of his character. He's very calm and patient—even in an emergency. And he rarely gets upset. In fact, I've only seen him get really angry once—about 20 years ago when I was 15. I came home at five in the morning and I didn't call to say I'd be late. We had a big argument and didn't speak to each other for a week! Except for that one time, we've always been really close.

Speaker 3
I work in a supermarket and I've been there for about two years. When I started, I got along really well with all my co-workers. They were all really nice, except one. This one girl—her name was Sarah—she was always unfriendly to me. I don't know why. Then I found out that she was saying bad things about me. She said I was lazy and a bad worker, that kind of thing. So one day I asked her, "What's the problem?" and she didn't say anything. Anyway, Sarah stopped working at the supermarket about a year ago. I don't know what she's doing now.

▶ 1.05 (Page 16)

Dialog 1
A: I've decided to stop smoking.
B: That's great! When did you decide this?
A: Last Monday. I haven't had a cigarette for three days.
B: Congratulations!
A: I had a cigar yesterday, though.
B: Oh.

Dialog 2
A: Have you seen my purse? I can't find it anywhere.
B: Your purse? I think I saw it on the table.
A: Ah, here it is. I've found it! Oh, no. Where are the car keys? I've lost the car keys now.
B: They're on the table. I put them there for you before breakfast.

UNIT 2 In the media

▶ 1.06 (Page 22)

I=Interviewer   J=Journalist (Allison)
I: Allison, I suppose the question most people ask is about the stories journalists write. What makes a good story?
J: Well, all good stories need certain components, certain factors that make them interesting for the reader. And there are two main types. The first type is when something strange has happened that readers can relate to. These are stories where you have ordinary people finding themselves in strange or funny situations, which we can all understand.

▶ 1.07 (Page 22)

I=Interviewer   J=Journalist (Allison)
I: Allison, I suppose the question most people ask is about the stories journalists write. What makes a good story?
J: Well, all good stories need certain components, certain factors that make them interesting for the reader. And there are two main types. The first type is when something strange has happened that readers can relate to. These are stories where you have ordinary people finding themselves in strange or funny situations, which we can all understand.
I: And the other type?
J: The other type concerns celebrities: movie stars, professional athletes, politicians. I think people enjoy reading about celebrities who have done something wrong because it shows their human side. Even if you're rich and famous, you can still make mistakes.
I: There's been a lot of criticism of journalists for writing too much about people's private lives. What's your opinion? Is it right to invade someone's private life for a story?
J: In my opinion, it depends on who it is and what is being reported. Is it right to follow regular people on vacation and take photos of them and their family? No, I don't think it is. But if these people are famous or they are spending public money—politicians, for example, we should definitely check what they're doing.
I: So it depends on each individual case?
J: I think so, yes.
I: But what do you think of those newspapers who follow celebrities 24 hours a day and take pictures of them?

J: Well, there are different types of newspapers. Some are full of gossip and celebrity news. They don't contain serious journalism. They sell because the public wants to see famous people in their private moments.

I: Doesn't that seem wrong to you?

J: I'm not sure about that. I don't think so. If you become a movie star or a celebrity, you know what's going to happen to your life. And many celebrities need that publicity to keep them in the public eye. Celebrities need photographers and photographers need celebrities.

I: I'm sure the photographers would agree with you.

J: Definitely.

▶ 1.08 (Page 22)

Speaker 1
I think political news is boring.

Speaker 2
In my opinion, newspapers should be free.

Speaker 3
I don't like watching sports. There's too much of it on television.

Speaker 4
I don't think the Internet has changed the world.

Speaker 5
Journalists shouldn't write about people's private lives.

▶ 1.09 (Page 23)

Speaker 1: TV show producer
The worst thing is technical problems. Everyone is in the studio, and suddenly it all goes black and people are running around trying to work out what the problem is, and fix it. A major technical problem can be the microphone. Maybe it isn't working properly or you can't hear someone because the microphone is in their jacket, and all you can hear is their clothes moving. Or people forget to take the microphone off when they finish. One time that happened, the audience could hear a man we had just interviewed complaining about the show and the producer. Obviously he didn't know that 300 people were listening to him, including me!

Speaker 2: News reporter
Sometimes I have to read bad news, and that can be very difficult. And I hate it when there are difficult names that I can't pronounce. Names of places you've never heard of. And it's also hard trying to think of what to wear every day.

Speaker 3: TV talk show host
It's difficult when you're tired and you keep making mistakes. I was interviewing a woman the other day, and I kept getting her name wrong. It was really embarrassing. Or sometimes the person you are interviewing gets nervous, and they don't say anything. You keep asking questions, but there's just silence. That's terrible. Or if they say something funny, and you start laughing, and then you can't stop.

Speaker 4: Soap opera actress
The worst thing is when you forget your lines. Everything else is perfect, the lights, the sound, the other actors, but you can't remember what you're supposed to say. That's very embarrassing. Or if the furniture falls down or breaks. I closed a door the other day, and the window fell off!

▶ 1.10 (Page 23)

Dialog 1
A: What's the matter?
B: The printer's broken again.
A: Should I call the IT department?

Dialog 2
A: Oh no! My computer keeps freezing!
B: Try turning it off and on again.
A: Thanks.

Dialog 3
A: What's the matter?
B: The copier isn't working. I think it's out of paper.
A: Don't worry. I'll deal with it.

▶ 1.12 (Page 27)

1. The bank robbers escaped.
2. She saved the young boy.
3. They waited for her for an hour.
4. Who delivered this package?
5. She spent all the money she inherited
6. We all helped them to do it.

UNIT 3 Home sweet home

▶ 1.13 (Page 33)

Dialog 1: The Miller family
I=Interviewer   D=David   L=Linda
I: So, David, are you ready for Brazil?
D: Yes, I think so. We've always wanted to visit. Brazil has such a rich culture. I want our daughters to experience that while they're young, even though, as teenagers, they'll probably just want to sit outside and enjoy the sun!
L: We're going to see the old churches and historic buildings. And I read that Ouro Preto has some great restaurants. David and I love Brazilian food, so we are going to try all the local dishes like churrasco and feijoada.
D: So basically, we're going to enjoy the culture. I really hope this'll be the vacation of a lifetime for us.

Dialog 2: The Costa family
I=Interviewer   P=Paula   R=Ricardo
I: So how do you feel about the house swap, Paula?
P: Oh, I can't wait. I can hardly believe we're spending more than a month in Toronto. We've never been there before.
I: I'm sure you'll love it. What are you going to do while you're there, Ricardo?
R: We're going to see all the sights and the museums . . .
P: And I'm going to do lots of shopping.
I: Oh, there are some wonderful shopping areas in Toronto. I'll give you the address of a great outlet mall. You can get incredible deals on clothes and shoes.
R: And we're visiting some old friends in Ottawa on June 3rd.
P: I think they'll have nice stores there, too, and of course . . .

▶ 1.14 (Page 34)

Dialog 1: Paula Costa
I=Interviewer   P=Paula
I: Hi Paula. So how was Toronto?
P: Well Toronto was fantastic, but the house was a disaster.
I: Oh, no. Why was that?
P: First of all, it was in the middle of nowhere. It was a long way from the center of the city and very difficult to find. We got completely lost looking for it. In the end we had to ask a taxi driver to take us there, which was very expensive. And when we went inside, my goodness, it was so old and dark. I don't think they had changed anything in that house for 30 years. It was like something out of a movie. Nothing worked. Even the air conditioner didn't work, and there was no hot water in the shower. Anyway, I was really disappointed. We're going to complain to the company. We'll ask them about the air conditioner and why the information on the website was wrong and we'll also ask them . . .

Dialog 2: David Miller
I=Interviewer   D=David
I: How was Brazil?
D: I have to be honest with you. Brazil was fabulous. But our apartment was not so good.
I: Uh oh. What was the problem?
D: Well, the main problem was it was too small. The girls wanted to stay in the single room together, but it was more like a closet than a room. It was tiny! And it was the biggest room in the apartment! And it was so hot, and there was no fan, so we were always arguing. Also the mosquitoes were terrible, so it was really hard to sleep at night. And downstairs there was a bar that played loud music until four in the morning. I think the only reason the area was quiet during the day is because everyone was sleeping after being up all night! And my daughters refused to do the things I wanted to do. All they wanted to do was try and get a suntan. They didn't want to learn anything about the culture, or eat the delicious food. They just wanted fast food!
At the end of the month, I was so glad to get home. We'd actually love to visit Brazil again, but I am never going to do another home swap!

▶ 1.15 (Page 35)

T=Tomofumi   C=Claudia
T: So, Claudia, how was the first day of your trip?
C: Incredible. I had such a great time yesterday!
T: What have you done so far?
C: Well, yesterday morning I took the subway by myself and did a little shopping.
T: Did you have any trouble finding your way?
C: No, not at all. The subway is really easy to use. All the signs are in English. And it's so clean! I didn't see even a single piece of garbage! There was one thing that really surprised me, though.

T: What's that?

C: On my way back to the hotel, the subway was really crowded. At first it didn't look like everyone was going to fit into the train. But then a train employee appeared wearing white gloves and he gently pushed people into the car!

T: Ah, yes. They're called "oshiya" or "pushers." The subway is so crowded during rush hours in Tokyo. The oshiya help keep people moving into the subway cars so the doors can close.

C: Oh, I see. That makes sense, actually. But I don't think that would be very popular back home in Mexico!

T: So, did you make it off the subway?

C: I did! And the streets were almost as busy! Everywhere you looked there was something interesting to see. I stopped to watch some guys dancing to rock music in a park.

T: And how was the shopping?

C: It was amazing! The buildings and stores are so new and fashionable. I spent hours in this enormous department store that has ten floors!

T: Did you find any bargains?

C: Well, I bought some really cute souvenirs for my family. But they weren't cheap. I think maybe I'd better stay away from the department stores!

▶ **1.16** **(Page 38)**

washing machine   air conditioner
DVD player   cell phone   burglar alarm
alarm clock

▶ **1.17** **(Page 40)**

Call one
R=Receptionist   S=Mr. Sharp

R: Davies Electronics.

S: Hello I'd like to speak to Mrs. Davies, please.

R: May I ask who's calling, please?

S: Sure, It's Ken Sharp.

R: Thank you. I'm afraid she's not in the office at the moment, Mr. Sharp. Can I take a message?

S: Yes. Could you ask her to call me back? It's about Friday's meeting.

R: Yes, of course. Can I have your number?

S: It's 202-555-8226.

R: That's 202-555-8226. I'll give her your message.

S: Thank you.

R: Goodbye.

S: Goodbye.

Call two
R=Receptionist   G=Gabriella Jones

R: Clanner Fabrics. Robert speaking.

G: Hi. This is Gabriella Jones from Accounts. Can I speak to Paul, please?

R: One moment please. I'm sorry. Paul is on another line.

G: Can I leave a message?

R: Yes, of course.

G: Can you have him call me at extension 466? I'm in the Accounts Department.

R: OK, no problem.

G: Thanks.

Call three
R=Receptionist   A=Andrea Jackson

R: Good morning. Juarez and Son. How can I help you?

A: Good morning. Can you put me through to Ricardo Villas?

R: Yes. May I ask who's calling?

A: It's Andrea Jackson.

R: Anthea Jackson?

A: No, Andrea Jackson.

R: Thank you. I'm afraid he's not at his desk at the moment. Would you like to leave a message?

A: Yes. Could you ask Mr. Villas to fax me an invoice?

R: Fax you an invoice. Does he have your fax number, Ms. Jackson?

A: No, it's 555-3149.

R: OK. I'll leave a message for him. The number's 555-3149. Is that right?

A: That's right. Thanks. Goodbye.

R: Goodbye.

UNIT 4 Wealth

▶ **1.18** **(Page 45)**

Frank Abagnale, a good-looking young man from England, pretended to be first a pilot, then a doctor, and then a lawyer. For five years he traveled the world for free, stayed in expensive hotels, and had relationships with beautiful women. Furthermore, by the age of 21 he had tricked and cheated his way to $250 million.

In the golden age of James Bond, Abagnale really was an international man of mystery. He was wanted by the FBI and Interpol (International Police) in 26 cities. Abagnale's charm was his most important tool. He dressed well and everybody believed everything he said. Leonardo DiCaprio, who plays Frank Abagnale in the film *Catch Me if You Can,* said, "Frank Abagnale is one of the greatest actors who has walked the earth."

Abagnale was a lonely child. When his German mother divorced his father, Abagnale had to choose which parent to live with. Instead, he ran away from home and began his life as an international trickster. He got a Pan Am pilot's uniform by saying that his was stolen and that he had an urgent flight. This allowed him to stay in any hotel he wanted. Pan Am always paid the bill. What's more, he even pretended to be baseball player and played for a professional team for a year.

Abagnale broke the law constantly, but he never went to prison until he was finally caught in the United States. Despite his crimes, Abagnale never had any enemies.

These days Abagnale doesn't need to trick anybody: he is a successful consultant. He advises companies on how to cheat their customers, and he also lectures at the FBI Academy. He wrote his autobiography in the 1970s and sold the movie rights for $250,000.

▶ **1.19** **(Page 46)**

C=Mr. Charming   W=Woman   M=Man

1.

C: What a beautiful dress! Haven't I seen you before? You work in fashion, don't you?

W: Yes, I do. We met at a fashion show in Tokyo.

2.

M: Are you familiar with my work?

C: I've read all your books. You've just written a new one, haven't you?

M: Yes, I have. It's about a movie star.

3.

C: I love lobster! The food is delicious here, isn't it?

W: Yes, it is. But I prefer caviar.

▶ **1.20** **(Page 47)**

Thank you for coming. It's good to see so many young entrepreneurs here. Today I'm going to talk about how to get rich. The writer F. Scott Fitzgerald once wrote, "Let me tell you about the very rich. They are different from you and me." He's right. The super-rich have a number of personal qualities that make them different. But they aren't all good qualities. Here are some ideas for you entrepreneurs who want to become wealthy.

▶ **1.21** **(Page 47)**

Here are some ideas for you entrepreneurs who want to get rich. The first thing is, be cheap. You shouldn't be too generous. John Paul Getty, one of the richest men in history, put payphones in the bedrooms of his house so that his friends couldn't make free phone calls.

Number two. You should start early. Really rich people know they want to be rich even when they are children. Matthew Freud sold mice to his school friends. He said he would be a millionaire by the time he was 25 years old. He was right.

Number three. Don't be too extravagant. You can't waste your money on stupid things. Bill Gates doesn't wear a suit. He doesn't care about looking good because he doesn't have to look good. If you spend all your money on expensive suits and luxury vacations, you will probably never be rich.

Number four. Be confident. You must believe in yourself. Everyone has great ideas, but 99.9 percent of us never do anything about them.

Donald Trump says, "Confidence can get you where you want to go, and getting there is a daily process. It's so much easier when you feel good about yourself, your abilities, and talents."

Number five. You have to work hard. Work long hours. This is the most important thing. No one ever got rich by sleeping half the day. Sam Walton, the founder of Walmart, would start his workday at three or four o'clock. That's 3:00 or 4:00 in the morning. Most of his executives would arrive at 5:00 A.M. By the time their competitors had poured their first cup of coffee at 9:00 A.M., the Walmart executives had been at their desks and in meetings for over four hours.

Number six. Think big. Be ambitious. You shouldn't think about the limits of your business. Sell yourself to the world, not only your home town. Of course there are a lot of other . . .

▶ **1.23** **(Page 51)**

succeed   fail   reward   punish   buy
sell   produce   consume   success
failure   reward   punishment   buyer
seller   producer   consumer

UNIT 5 Spare time

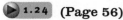 **1.24** (Page 56)

Speaker 1
I've been taking classes in origami for three months. Basically, you learn how to make beautiful objects using paper. It's an ancient Japanese art and I really love it. It's very creative, and I've made lots of beautiful things already, like birds and other animals.

Speaker 2
Well, my hobby is cooking. I think it's actually quite creative. I've made up a lot of my own recipes and people say I'm a good cook. I've been trying to open my own restaurant for the last few years but I don't have the money yet. But it's something I'll definitely do in the future.

Speaker 3
I think you have to be creative to take care of children. We do all kinds of things: drawing, playing games, music. You know, I've been playing with my three children this morning—that's why the room's a mess— and we've invented a new game. And tomorrow there'll be another new game.

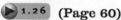 **1.25** (Page 60)

1. I saw the man.
2. She lost her hat.
3. I like the red.
4. He ran after the car.

1.26 (Page 60)

I=Interviewer   H=Hannah
I: Hannah, did it surprise you how you spend your free time?
H: Yeah, I didn't expect to see these results at all. Um . . . I'm a film-maker, so I think it's normal to spend a lot of time going to the movies and watching DVDs, but a lot of other things surprised me.
I: For example?
H: For example, I spend 8 percent of my free time shopping. Well, I can't stand shopping. It drives me crazy.
I: Really?
H: Yeah, and housework—I don't mind doing housework, but it's not very interesting and I'd prefer to do less of that kind of thing. Also I noticed that I spend 15 percent of my time watching TV and only 10 percent reading, which surprises me because I enjoy reading and I always look forward to starting a new book.
I: You don't like TV so much?
H: Well, most TV is like junk food for the brain and I think I should watch less. Other things . . . um . . . I love cooking, and I try to prepare a healthy meal at least four nights a week. And I often invite friends over to have dinner, so it doesn't surprise me that I spend 7 percent of my time cooking and eating.
I: Is there anything you'd really like to change?
H: Um . . . I never manage to do much exercise. I'd really like to go running every day just for half an hour, but I never seem to find the time. So that's one thing I'd like to change.

1.27 (Page 64)

A: Have you been to La Pescada, that new restaurant downtown?
B: No. Where is it?
A: It's on Market Street, near the bookstore.
B: Is it any good?
A: It's incredible. I went there last night. It's Argentinian, and it has a great atmosphere—very lively. They have live music and serve a very traditional menu with lots of meat and fish. The chef is from Argentina, so he makes sure that all the meat is really fresh and good quality. They serve huge steaks with a spicy salsa and lots of delicious vegetables. And the best thing about it is that the prices are very reasonable. Oh, and the waiters are really friendly and good-looking too! Next time you're downtown, you have to go. You'll love it!

1.28 (Page 66)

I am going to tell you about Capoeira. Capoeira originated in Brazil, where it was started by the African slaves. It's a kind of martial art, but it's also like a dance. To do Capoeira you need to be very fit and strong, and you should have good control of your body. You often have to use your hands to balance. Everyone sits around in a circle, singing and playing music, and two people fight in the center. To fight the other person you kick with your feet, but nowadays, there is no contact. As soon as you see the other person's hand or foot coming toward you, you have to move away quickly. You must be careful the other person doesn't kick you. If the other person kicks you, then you lose.
Afterward, you can relax and talk about the fight. And we often spend the evening together, listening to music. I have been doing Capoeira for three years. I have improved a lot since I first started, and now I wear a green belt. In the future, I would like to become a trainer and teach other people about this beautiful sport.

UNIT 6 Travel tales

2.02 (Page 70)

Speaker 1
This photo shows me walking along the Great Wall of China. It was early in the morning, so there weren't a lot of people there. The wall climbs up and over all of these hills. It's a difficult walk! From the tower in the background, you can see the mountains and the wall stretching out as far as you can see. Parts of the wall looked like they had been built in the clouds. I had already been in Beijing for one week, and before I left, I wanted to see the wall. I was very excited because I had heard that you can see this wall from the moon, and I wanted to see it for myself.

Speaker 2
This is a photo of me at the Grand Canyon. I went there with my family—all six of us. I took this photo after we'd been hiking for a few hours. We felt very happy to be there because we had heard about the canyon, how beautiful it was. Some friends had told us how amazing it was but we'd never expected to see it ourselves. So it was cool to see it in real life. It was huge. We walked for several hours, and afterward we just sat quietly. It was a very silent place and so beautiful.

Speaker 3
We took a train up the mountain and then we took a bus, and we were very high up, and then we walked to Machu Picchu. Far below us there was a river. We were very near the clouds and there were mountains covered in trees. We kept walking past a few stone huts and waiting to see the great ruin. We were very excited. We'd always wanted to see Machu Picchu. I'd heard that some people had started crying when they first saw the city because it's such an incredible sight. Anyway, eventually we got to a place where we could see all of the city. The stone ruins were so powerful and we couldn't believe that the people actually built this city on the top of a mountain. It really was amazing. I took this photo when I first saw the city, just after we'd arrived.

2.03 (Page 71)

Dialog 1
A: I'd like two tickets to Vancouver, please.
B: One way or round trip?
A: Round trip, please.
B: That's twenty-two thirty, please.
A: Thank you. Could you tell me what time the next train leaves?
B: Two fifteen. But there are some delays. You need to listen to the announcements.
A: OK! Thanks.

Dialog 2
A: Excuse me. How do we get to the National History Museum?
B: Um . . . right. The quickest thing to do is to take the 31 bus to Grafton Street, and then ask again.
A: Is it far from Grafton Street?
B: No, it's a short walk from there. I think it's about five minutes' walk.
A: OK. Thank you.
B: But it's closed at the moment.
A: Oh! Thank you anyway.

Dialog 3
A: Excuse me. Is there a post office near here?
B: Yes, there's one just down the road. Just go straight, and it's on your left.
A: Thank you.
B: But it's closed now. You need to go before 6 o'clock.
A: Oh, OK! Thanks.

Dialog 4
A: Excuse me. Does this bus go to Sydney Harbor?
B: No, this one's for the airport. You need the 356.
A: OK, thanks.
B: But you need to go to the bus stop across the road.
A: Across the road?
B: That's right. There's a bus every 15 minutes I think.
A: Great. Thanks for your help.
B: No worries.

Dialog 5

A: Two student tickets, please.

B: Do you have a student ID?

A: Yes. One moment. Oh. I can't find it. I think I left it at my hotel.

B: Then I'm afraid you'll have to pay the full admission. That'll be nineteen dollars please.

A: Nineteen dollars! OK. Thanks.

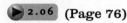 **(Page 71)**

1. What time does the museum open?
2. Is there a bank near here?
3. Can you recommend a good restaurant?
4. How much is a round trip ticket to the city center?
5. Does this bus go to the airport?
6. Excuse me. Could you tell me what time the train leaves?
7. Excuse me. Do you know where platform 1 is?
8. Can you tell me the way to the station, please?
9. Just go straight. It's on your left.

2.06 (Page 76)

Dialog 1

A: This diver finds 15 wedding rings a year.

B: Does he?

A: And he returns most of them.

B: How interesting!

Dialog 2

A: A dog went home alone from India to Scotland.

B: Really? How?

A: It traveled by boat and, after months at sea, it ran home.

B: Huh. That's amazing!

Dialog 3

A: I read an amazing story about a family that was sailing.

B: Did you? What happened?

A: A whale jumped onto their boat.

B: Really? Where?

A: Near Australia.

Dialog 4

A: Karen Goode found a ring she'd lost ten years ago.

B: Did she? How?

A: It was on the same beach.

B: That's incredible!

UNIT 7 Lifelong learning

2.08 (Page 80)

Speaker 1

My art teacher at college had a strange way of teaching us to draw faces. It was learning by doing. He told us to sit opposite a partner and draw the person's face without looking. He tied a scarf around your head, so you couldn't see the paper you were drawing on. Also, you had to keep the pencil on the paper all the time, so the picture was just one line. There were some very funny faces. But it did help you not to feel embarrassed.

Speaker 2

When I was learning the piano, my teacher told me to hold an orange in each hand as I played. It was supposed to help the position of your hand on the keyboard, but it was very difficult.

Speaker 3

They say that practice makes perfect. Well, my sister wanted desperately to learn to ride a bicycle, but nobody had time to teach her. One day I found her sitting on the bicycle trying to balance it without moving. "I am practicing," she said. "When I can do it standing still, then I'll be ready to start moving forward."

Speaker 4

When I was studying Spanish with my roommate, she wrote the names of all the words she knew in Spanish on pieces of paper and stuck them around the apartment so that she could learn them by heart. She wrote lists of verbs and tenses and put them in the bathroom and on the bedroom wall. Everywhere you went, you saw Spanish on the walls. It was really useful.

2.09 (Page 83)

A: Do you remember Mr. Halsworth, our history teacher in fifth grade?

B: Yeah! I do. A short guy with thick glasses. He was so boring and we always behaved so badly in his class, remember? We used to throw paper at him!

A: That's right. He used to shout so much he would get red in the face.

B: Poor man. I remember Mrs. Matthews— the music teacher. She was really beautiful, and she used to play us Mozart and teach us songs from Africa. I remember her lessons were so relaxing and enjoyable. She was inspiring.

A: Yeah. I really liked her. And she was so patient. Not like Madame Bouchier, the French teacher! She was frightening! I didn't use to like her lessons at all. She used to tell me to sit at the front of the class, right under her nose, and ask me all the most difficult questions. And if you failed a test, or forgot to do your homework, she would punish you. Oh, and how about Mr. Ford, the social studies teacher?

B: He was great!

A: He was so open-minded, wasn't he? He used to teach us all about different cultures of the world and he was also interested in astronomy, so we'd learn about the stars, too. He was very knowledgeable.

B: And he never lost his temper, not even when we used to . . .

2.11 (Page 88)

1. I could do it.
2. He wasn't able to stop.
3. I couldn't run fast.
4. They were able to play.
5. We couldn't see it.
6. Were you able to go?

2.12 (Page 90)

This happened when I was about eight or nine. I went to a large school in the city. We didn't know anything about the countryside—all we knew about was the city. So one day my teacher decided to take the class to the countryside. It was a two-hour journey in the school bus, and when we got there, we looked at trees and nature and birds and things like that. It was a beautiful sunny day. Anyway, on the final part of the trip, in the afternoon, we went horseback riding. Now, it was the first time most of us had even seen a horse, and we had to get on it and ride. And I remember getting on this huge horse. They were really, really big. Everyone else was moving really slowly on these horses. And, of course, what did my horse do? It decided to run off, with me on top of it. At first it didn't go too fast. But all of a sudden it started galloping. So there I was screaming and shouting, with my arms around this horse, and it just wouldn't stop. I don't know how I didn't fall off. And the whole class was laughing at me. Eventually, I managed to stop it. Afterwards I was so frightened I was shaking for like an hour. It was the most embarrassing and frightening experience. I'll never forget it. I learned that horses and I don't go together, and I've never been on a horse since!

UNIT 8 Making changes

2.13 (Page 94)

Speaker 1: Gabriel

Mexico City has too many cars, so it's really polluted. So if I could change one thing, I'd have a law against all the traffic. I'd stop cars from going into the city center.

Speaker 2: Luciana

I'd improve the facilities for disabled people. People in wheelchairs have real problems because of the roads and pavements. Even in public buildings sometimes there are no elevators so they can't use the rooms on the higher floors.

Speaker 3: Clive

There's no peace and quiet here. All the noise and mess is caused by these students. They scream and shout every night. So I would make some new laws against all the noise so we could get some sleep!

Speaker 4: Min-Ji

Because of the stupid laws here, everybody builds these terrible buildings. They are really ugly, which means the city isn't so beautiful these days. If I were mayor, I would pass a law to stop these buildings.

▶ 2.14 (Page 95)

A: The biggest change? I think it's probably been medical progress. The situation has really improved. Luckily, doctors and scientists can cure so many diseases now that were just impossible when I was younger.

B: That's true.

A: Life-saving cures and operations have become more and more common. I'm sure in the future, disease won't be such a big problem, because we'll discover cures for most of the really bad diseases.

B: I don't know about that. There are still no cures for some of the most common diseases, like the flu. And in developing countries, there isn't enough money to pay for some of the cures, so the situation hasn't changed.

A: Yes, that is a problem.

B: No, I think that the biggest change has been the change in lifestyle. It's gotten much worse.

A: Worse? How?

B: People work too much now, and unfortunately they don't have time to spend with their families. And when people have free time, they just watch TV. So not surprisingly, people are getting fatter. They're always too busy to cook properly, so they eat fast food and . . .

▶ 2.15 (Page 98)

Speaker 1: Mei Ling
My father wanted me to work in the family business in China, like my brothers did, but I was never interested in that. I had always dreamed of going to study in another country, to study art. So when I finished school, I applied, and I was admitted to a university in Paris. It was a big decision to come here, leaving my family and friends and coming to this country. Everything is so different here but it has worked out very well. I met my fiancé, Jun, here, and we are planning to get married when I finish my degree. So I'm happy I came here. I wouldn't have met Jun if I hadn't come to France!

Speaker 2: Sarah
My boyfriend was working nights as a lorry driver. We weren't very happy because we didn't really see each other. Then we went on holiday to Italy, and while we were there, we saw this old olive farm for sale. It needed lots of work doing to it, but it was beautiful, and we just fell in love with the house the moment we saw it. We came back to England, sold our house, left our jobs, and said good-bye to our friends. Two months later, we drove down to Italy to start our new life growing olives to make olive oil. It was very hard for the first year and we nearly changed our minds. We didn't have much money, and we knew nothing about farming olives or how to run our own business. But now things are much better, and we enjoy working together. I am glad we didn't have a change of heart. If we'd gone back to England, we wouldn't have been happy.

Speaker 3: Roger
I stopped working a year ago, when we discovered Jack, our three-year-old son had a kidney problem. Before that, I just worked all the time. All I thought about was making money for my family. But when we discovered Jack was seriously ill, it changed our world completely. I decided to give up my job so that I could spend more time with him. Now I pick up the children from school every day, and we walk home through the park. It's been great to be with Jack, and now he has had an operation, which hopefully will mean that his life will go back to normal. And what about me? Well, I won't be able to get my old job back, so maybe I'll change careers and start my own business. But for me it was the right decision. If I'd stayed at work, I wouldn't have spent time with Jack when he really needed me.

UNIT 9 On the job

▶ 2.18 (Page 106)

Good afternoon, everybody. Today I'd like to tell you about our idea for a new business. We want to open a restaurant that serves food from all over the world. Our main idea is that the chefs cook food from 50 or 60 countries. The most important thing for us is that the food is great. We'll allow the chefs to choose the dishes and the menu will be very big, with something for everybody. We will employ three chefs and six waiters. We won't make the waiters wear a uniform, and they will have one special perk: we will let them eat free at our restaurant. To sum up, our restaurant will be small and friendly but with a great international menu. The name of the restaurant is World Food! Thank you for listening. Are there are any questions?

▶ 2.19 (Page 107)

Speaker 1
I find my manager really annoying. She always stops by my desk at the end of the day and gives me more work to do. Naturally, it all has to be finished by the next day. It makes it very hard for me to organize my time.

Speaker 2
I am very pleased to work for Anya. She's a great boss and very understanding. For instance, when my wife was in the hospital, she sent her flowers. And when I was feeling worried about it, she sent me home for the day. I didn't have to ask because she knows how you feel before you say anything.

Speaker 3
My supervisor can be really aggressive. If someone forgets to do something, he really shouts. Sometimes he even throws things around the office. It can be very frightening.

Speaker 4
It's very exciting to work with Michael because he has so much energy and enthusiasm. He has a lot of new ideas for the company, and he involves other people so that everyone's opinion is included. Work never gets boring because he is always challenging us to try new things.

▶ 2.20 (Page 109)

I=Interviewer W=Mr. Wilkins

I: So, Mr. Wilkins, you've applied for a management position. Let me ask you a few questions.

W: Of course.

I: First of all, are you good at listening to people?

W: Yes, I think so. People often talk to me about their problems and ask me for advice. So yes.

I: Their problems? That's interesting. And can you usually find solutions to difficult problems?

W: Well, actually, not always. No. I usually ask other people for their ideas. If there's a problem at work, for example, I ask my co-workers for ideas, and then try a few different solutions to see which one works.

I: That's good. So you listen to other people's ideas?

W: That's right.

I: And what do you think are your strengths and weaknesses?

W: Well, I'd say that my strengths are that I work very hard. I'm very motivated. And I'm good with people, so I get along well with my co-workers. My weakness is probably that I'm a bit disorganized. My desk is always a mess, and I tend to arrive late for meetings.

I: I see. And do you work well under pressure?

W: Yes. Very well. I'm a calm person by nature, so if there's a problem I don't panic. As I said before, I like to work hard, so if there's a lot of work to do, I'm happy to just keep working until it's finished. I'll get up very early in the morning, or just work all night until the job's done. That's not a problem.

I: OK. And do you like working on your own?

W: Um . . . that's a difficult one. I like working with people, as I said. That's the part of the job I enjoy most. But if there is a difficult document or report to write, then I work well on my own. Sometimes I'll work from home so that there are no interruptions, so then I work on my own.

I: That's great. Well, thank you for taking the time to come and see us Mr. Wilkins . . .

▶ 2.21 (Page 112)

Speaker 1: Flight attendant
You have to be good at dealing with people. Some people get nervous about flying, or they feel sick, so you need to comfort them. Or sometimes there are arguments between passengers, so you need to listen to people and solve these types of problems. Also, sometimes you have to persuade people to do things they don't want to do, like sit in a different seat or check their carry-on bags. It's useful to speak more than one language. And of course you have to like traveling! I travel thousands of miles every week.

Speaker 2: Office manager
I found that you needed to prioritize. There were so many things to do—you had to say, "This is important. I'll do this first." And then as manager you had to delegate, find other people to do some of the jobs. We worked under a lot of pressure in my office. Sometimes I couldn't sleep because of all the stress. That was fairly common. Other things: well, it was useful to be able to type fast. And we used a whole range of computer software. So, yeah it was kind of one of those jobs . . .

Speaker 3: Medical scientist
You had to work accurately. You couldn't make mistakes. And also you had to be very good with numbers. It was different when I was doing the job, but these days they use a lot of computer software in the laboratory. In fact, most medical science work is done by computer. And this helps with solving problems because often you don't get the result you're looking for, and you don't know why.

Speaker 4: Bus driver
You need to be able to drive well obviously, and also to be patient. That's the most important thing. What else? Well, we sometimes get stuck in traffic jams. You know, it's a hot day and you're in the middle of the city, and you're stuck for an hour with the bus not moving. Well, people get angry—other drivers, passengers—so we have to deal with these people. And then sometimes we work irregular hours—at nights or early in the morning. That's a bit of a pain in the neck, but you know someone's gotta do it . . .

UNIT **10** Memories of you

 2.22 (Page 117)

A=Alicia J=Jack

A: Do you have a good memory?
J: I wish I did! My memory is terrible! I'm good at remembering things like appointments and meetings at work. That's fine. But I'm terrible with faces and names. It happens all the time that I meet people and I immediately forget their name.
A: Me, too. I'm hopeless. I can never remember faces. The other day I was walking along the street and this man came up and said hello. And I had no idea who he was.
J: Who was he?
A: He was my boss's husband.
J: Oops.
A: Very embarrassing. What about dates? Do you remember people's birthdays, that kind of thing?
J: Well, I'm OK with birthdays because I write them all down on my calendar. I wish I didn't have to, but . . . you know.
A: And phone numbers?
J: I can't even remember my own phone number half the time.
A: Personally, I wish I could remember things like writers' names or the names of songs. The other day I was talking about a novel I'd just finished. I wanted to recommend the book but I couldn't remember the author's name. I had a complete mental block!

J: What was the title of the book?
A: Um, I can't remember that either!

 2.23 (Page 118)

1. True! Brazilian Wish Ribbons have been around for hundreds of years. This tradition has spread around the world, and the ribbons are fashionable in addition to being a good luck charm.
2. True! The crane is a sacred creature in Japan, believed to live for a thousand years. A thousand actual origami paper cranes are a traditional wedding gift in Japan. The person who folds the cranes wishes a thousand years of happiness and good fortune to the couple.
3. True! If you stand or sit between two people who have the same first name, it is considered very lucky in Russia. This is not as hard as it sounds, since certain Russian first names are very common.
4. True! Grapes are believed to give good energy. It is very difficult, however, to eat the grapes so quickly. So people ring in the New Year with mouthfuls of grapes, which is very funny. To help people with their New Year's wishes, stores now sell skinless seedless grapes, which are easier to eat quickly.
5. False!
6. False!
7. True! But be careful. This can be dangerous when the tunnel or bridge is very long or if there is a lot of traffic! The wish may not be worth it if your face turns blue and your palms start to sweat.
8. False!

▶ **2.24** (Page 119)

Speaker 1
Frida Kahlo was a gifted painter from Mexico. She was famous for her amazing and unusual paintings. At age 18, she was involved in a serious accident in which she nearly died. But she was determined to survive and made a remarkable recovery. Many people admired her for her colorful and lively personality.

Speaker 2
Mother Teresa dedicated her life to helping street children and sick people in India. She started the Missionaries of Charity to help people in need. Her hard work and dedication inspired many other people to start caring for others. Now over 1 million people work for her charities in more than 40 countries.

Speaker 3
Marie Curie was a brilliant scientist. Originally from Poland, she went to study in France and worked at the Sorbonne University with her husband, Pierre. Together, they discovered radiation. She won the Nobel Prize in 1903 and 1911.

Speaker 4
Marilyn Monroe was a talented actress who was loved by people all over the world. She overcame many problems in her life to become one of the 20th century's greatest cultural icons. Although she died quite young, she had already starred in 30 films during her career and is particularly remembered for her charm and beauty.

▶ **2.26** (Page 122)

Dialog 1
M=Man
M: So, thank you very much for coming, everybody. I hope you found the talks interesting and useful. If you want any more information, you can find us on our website. The address is in the program, so do send us an email. Thank you and goodbye.

Dialog 2
F=Father D=Daughter
F: OK, you've got everything? Passport, ticket, money.
D: Yeah, I think so . . .
F: Do you have the address where you're staying?
D: Yes.
F: Your cell phone?
D: Yeah, it's right here.
F: So, you'll give us a call when you arrive?
D: Yeah, it'll probably be late tonight.
F: OK, have a safe trip.
D: Thanks, Dad.
F: See you in a couple of weeks.
D: Two weeks. OK, bye.
F: Bye, darling.

Dialog 3
M=Man W=Woman
M: Going home?
W: Yep. Just finished that report.
M: Have a good weekend.
W: You too. Bye.
M: Bye.

Dialog 4
M=Man W=Woman
M: Thanks for everything. I really enjoyed it.
W: You're welcome. Come back any time.
M: Thanks a lot.
W: Maybe see you next weekend. There's a party at Joe's.
M: Oh, OK, yeah, sounds good. I'll give you a call. Bye.
W: Take care.